D0456736

ALSO BY LAURA DOYLE

*The Surrendered Wife:*
*A Practical Guide to Finding*
*Intimacy, Passion, and Peace with a Man*

# THE SURRENDERED SINGLE

## A PRACTICAL GUIDE TO ATTRACTING AND MARRYING THE MAN WHO'S RIGHT FOR YOU

LAURA DOYLE

A Fireside Book
Published by Simon & Schuster
New York London Toronto Sydney

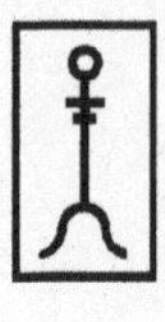

FIRESIDE
Rockefeller Center
1230 Avenue of the Americas
New York, NY 10020



For information about special discounts for bulk purchases,
please contact Simon & Schuster Special Sales:
1-800-456-6798 or business@simonandschuster.com

Designed by William Ruoto

Manufactured in the United States of America

10 9 8 7 6 5 4

Library of Congress Cataloging-in-Publication Data

Doyle, Laura.

The surrendered single: a practical guide to attracting and marrying the man who's right for you/Laura Doyle.

p. cm.

1. Dating (Social customs). 2. Mate selection. 3. Single women—Psychology. 4. Single women—Conduct of life. 5. Control (Psychology). I. Title.

HQ801.D758 2002
646.7'7—dc21 2002017558

ISBN 978-0-7432-1789-7

# Acknowledgments

Special thanks to Kay, Julia, Rachel, Anna, Melinda, Casey, Robin, Heatheryn, Jebra, and Loretta for being the first to try surrendered dating.

I have such gratitude for my terrific editor, Doris Cooper, for helping me say what I mean and having faith in me.

I'm also grateful to Christine Gordon for her intuitive, honest editing.

Special thanks to Jimmy Vines, the world's best agent.

Most of all, I appreciate my husband, John, who supported me through the process of writing this book in every way imaginable. I couldn't have done it without him.

For hopeful single women everywhere.

# CONTENTS

# Introduction: The Way You Always Wanted Things to Happen

*For one human being to love another: that is perhaps the most difficult of our tasks; the ultimate, the last test and proof, the work for which all other work is but preparation.*

—Rainer Maria Rilke

What is a Surrendered Single? And just what is she surrendering—and to whom?

A Surrendered Single recognizes that if she wants to attract the man with whom she can develop intimacy, she cannot control relationships. She cannot determine *who* asks her out, *how* he'll do it, *when* he'll call or e-mail, or if he'll commit to her. A Surrendered Single may have unwittingly been trying to control, manipulate, and force relationships previously, but no more.

She doesn't hunt for Mr. Right—she attracts him.

She's purposely quiet on first dates so she can learn more about him and stay with her own feelings and intuition about what he reveals.

She relinquishes her checklist of qualities she thinks she requires in a man. Then she acknowledges that she can be blissfully happy with an imperfect man and that she will definitely be lonely without one.

Surrendering is about following some basic principles that will help you change your habits and attitudes about dating. It is terrifying, because at times you will feel vulnerable. But the results are grand: Your fears will melt. You will discover amazing, available men. You will feel adored. You'll stop going it alone.

You will find intimacy with a good man.

## Surrender Control, Find Your Faith

There's a constant in romance: You can't control when, where, or how you fall in love. You can't even control with *whom* you fall in love. The chemistry and mystery of love are unpredictable.

Every story of how couples first met includes the element of a pleasant surprise. They didn't expect to meet their mates then or there. Not on a Wednesday. Not at the paint store. Not over nachos or during the seventh-inning stretch at a baseball game.

Marla didn't intend to fall in love with her friend's coworker, but now they're happily married with a baby. Had Jessica known she would meet her future husband at the gym one day, she probably would have put on lipstick before she left the house. Sarah didn't anticipate meeting anybody at all for a while after breaking off an engagement, but mutual friends of the man she would later marry introduced them.

These women did not expect to find their soul mates when or how they did. Whether they knew it or not, however, they did have faith that somewhere in the universe was a man who was right for them. They simply had to be open to the possibility of encountering him.

That's all faith is—being open to the possibilities.

Maybe you think that's great for other women, but you don't believe that faith—which may seem maddeningly elusive—is going to win you a great romance.

Think again.

Having faith means you can let life surprise you. That doesn't mean that we are powerless, only that we embrace the unknown and stop being afraid of uncertainty.

It means liking the idea that the man of your dreams may look and sound nothing like the one you had imagined. Faith means that you keep your door open to dating, no matter how discouraged and frustrated you are, because you believe that ultimately the man who's right for you will walk through it.

For those of us who would like to have control over every aspect of our lives, this is hard to swallow. The unknown is disconcerting. Trekking forward willingly requires faith.

Part of what keeps you single is lack of faith. The other part is fear of the unknown.

# WHO'S AFRAID OF DATING?

> *A person usually has two reasons for doing something: a good reason and the real reason.*
>
> —THOMAS CARLYLE

Every strong single woman I know rolls her eyes when I suggest that lack of faith and fear are what keep her alone. She doesn't think of herself as scared. After all, she's built a career and a terrific circle of friends, stood up to dozens of men, and perhaps even raised a child alone. She is capable and hearty. What's more, she's through with "having faith" because it hasn't done a thing for her (or so she thinks). In fact, the very word is disconcerting to her. Truth is, her faith is as out of shape as her first little black dress and as worn as the fabulous heels she bought to go with it.

This is understandable. When we believe that something will happen but have no control over whether it does, the possibility of disappointment looms. What could be more disappointing than believing he's out there but never finding him? We'd be faced with thinking that there's something wrong with *us*.

To protect herself, the single woman does a funny little sidestep. She goes into the world with good intentions to find someone who has all the characteristics she wants in a partner. She makes a list of these characteristics by starting with what she knows will meet her parents' approval and what her friends will like. Unfortunately, her list is now both restrictive and irrelevant, since it has nothing to do with her own desires.

Each potential suitor is measured against his ability to fit into her complicated jigsaw puzzle of the perfect guy.

Of course, nobody fits.

She *thinks* she feels hopeless that there's "no one out there," but really the terror of risking her heart keeps her from acknowledging that *any* man might be right. Her good intentions cover her fear and keep her from having to muster up a critical ingredient for finding love: courage.

Nobody wants to have her heart broken, so it's sensible to want to protect yourself.

At the same time, repeatedly searching for a partner and never finding one feels awful. Since trying to control potential suitors by comparing them to a checklist guarantees you'll end up empty-handed, surrendering means throwing out that checklist and giving yourself a chance to attract the unexpected.

When we surrender, we relinquish inappropriate control and override the fear underneath so we can have the thing we crave the most—intimacy.

## Control and Intimacy Are Opposites

If you've been dating off and on but never stay in a relationship for long, you may be telling yourself that you've just never met the right man. Chances are, your fear is preventing you from standing still or being quiet long enough to find out if the men you date might be right for you. Perhaps your fear of heartbreak propels you to elicit affection, reassurance, and commitment to assuage your insecurities. Maybe you feel safer being physically intimate than emotionally vulnerable and so you relegate potential relationships to short-lived sexual flings.

This is all about control.

If you haven't gone out on a date in a long time, you might be telling yourself that men just don't approach you, when really you've been trying to control *who* asks you out. Maybe you've been so focused on a man who shows little interest that you're missing out on other opportunities to date. Avoiding eye contact with men, refusing offers for blind dates, and running off before a guy has a chance to get your phone number are examples of trying to protect yourself with control.

Maybe you're in a committed relationship and wishing your boyfriend would shape up in some way—be tidier, make more money, enhance the romance, or propose. It's easy—and tempting—to be the armchair quarterback of someone else's life, but it's in taking responsibility for our own happiness that we make ourselves available for an intimate relationship.

No matter how you try to control the prospects and relationships in your life, the result is the same: Loneliness and exhaustion set in where tenderness and romance belong.

## The Recipe for Loneliness and Exhaustion

After I published my first book, *The Surrendered Wife: A Practical Guide to Finding Intimacy, Passion, and Peace with a Man*, single women asked me how they could find an intimate, passionate relationship. These women, like me, recognized their tendencies to dominate and manipulate, and they identified with my message: Control is the enemy of intimacy.

These single women hated to admit it, but their urge to control left them feeling the same way I had felt while trying to dictate every aspect of my marriage: exhausted and alone. I realized that the solution for singles seeking love would be the same that it was for wives craving intimate marriages: surrender and find the romance and emotional connection. I started a Surrendered Singles workshop in my living room to help women apply the principles of surrendering to attracting the right man. (You can learn more about workshops in your area by calling 1-800-466-2028 or visiting www.surrenderedsingle.com.) Surrendering is a powerful way to foster intimacy, and I watched thousands of women heal their marriages by relinquishing control of others.

I could see that the competent professional women who came to my house on Tuesday nights were afraid. "I'd rather have two broken arms and two broken legs than have a broken heart again," one woman said. I saw that they had been trying to manage their fear by staying in control. They tried to control who approached them. They tried to control how their dates behaved. They tried to prevent heartbreak by looking for and finding some insurmountable obstacle to compatibility with perfectly good men. They even tried to deny that they wanted to be in relationships in the first place.

They did all of this because they felt vulnerable.

## My Favorite Defense

*For peace of mind, resign as general manager of the universe.*

—Anonymous

By definition, vulnerability makes you feel exposed, and therefore afraid. I understand this particularly well because I, too, was once terrified of vulnerability. My favorite antidote to it was control. I felt safer if I thought I could manipulate the outcome of every situation.

Women who try to protect themselves with control have suffered disappointments in the past. Maybe you've been through a tragic divorce or watched your parents split. Perhaps it was something less dramatic, but also painful, like having your first love break up with you for another girl. Such hurt prompts women to erroneously believe that we can prevent all future heartache if we manage everything properly.

Of course, it isn't so. First, the only thing that you will get from trying to manage the people around you is the guarantee that you will never find intimacy. Second, there are no guarantees against heartache. However, surrendering makes heartache much less likely. In chapter 21 I show you why this is so.

I almost ruined my marriage by "helping" my husband decide when to take a nap, how to get a bargain in Mexico, and which guitar amplifier to buy. Behind this control was fear: that he would be tired and cranky, pay too much money, or buy an amplifier that cluttered our house. The threat of almost losing a relationship that had once made me so happy propelled me to learn how to surrender—to accept that I couldn't change anyone but myself, and that trying to change my husband was not only wasting my time but also killing my marriage.

I also discovered that when I changed myself by becoming more vulnerable, my husband responded to me differently.

Vulnerability makes us approachable and attractive, because it's a gift to the person we're with. It's an unspoken compliment that says, "I trust you to be gentle when I put down my armor. I feel safe with you." When someone gives me such a gift, my instinct is to be tender so as to reassure her that I understand the honor. Vulnerability will draw me to someone in a way that appearing invincible never could. That's because I identify with the humanity and authenticity. To appear perfect is to keep up your defenses, which means others can't see and love the real you.

Once you have someone's empathy, there's only one way for them to respond: with compassion.

When we surrender control of who pursues us and how he does it, we clear the way for the relationship we always wanted.

## THE POWER OF A WOMAN

> *One of the oldest human needs is having someone to wonder where you are when you don't come home at night.*
>
> —MARGARET MEAD

Women often protect themselves from disappointment and vulnerability by flaunting their independence. How many times have you thought, *I don't need anybody to take care of me* or *I can handle this?* Strength is attractive, but hard-nosed independence sends a "get away" message.

This masculine persona can be effective—and appropriate—in a work environment, where forcefulness and toughness get the job done.

But you have another side to you—the feminine side—that's soft, tender, vulnerable, and receptive. That part of you wants to be taken out to dinner, walked home, asked about, thought of, caressed, and just plain taken care of. It's the part of you that relishes feeling protected and cherished. These are undeniable feminine qualities. Since femininity is what men are fundamentally drawn to, those are the qualities that will attract a man who's right for you. Surrendering means acknowledging that you are a woman, with a feminine mind, body, and spirit.

Taking a feminine approach to dating means that when you leave the workplace (or even when you're interacting on a social level in the workplace), you turn off your ambition and your bossiness, and you relax into your feminine grace. You have the power to magnetize men with your manner, your scent, your body, and your voice. These will serve you far better in the dating arena than a know-it-all attitude or toughness.

Revealing your feminine qualities allows a man to show his strengths, too. For instance, when you let him treat you, you give him the opportunity to demonstrate his generosity and ability to please you. This makes him feel proud and happy to be with you. If you dismiss his offers in the name of self-sufficiency, you reject *him*. If you try to one-up him or even the score, you're competing with him as if you were one of the guys, instead of luxuriating in the adoration and affection he offers because you are a woman. Now because he feels superfluous, he wonders why he should bother trying to do anything for you.

Pleasing a woman makes a man feel more masculine and good about himself. Men want to see your soft side so they can show their strength. By being feminine, we allow our man's masculinity to shine.

Men and women really are infinitely different, and you'll enjoy the foil of his masculinity to your femininity if you surrender to both.

James Thurber wrote, "I love the idea of there being two sexes, don't you?"

# "Surrender" Really Is the Right Word

> *Eventually I lost interest in trying to control . . . to make things happen in a way that I thought I wanted them to be. I began to practice surrendering to the universe and finding out what "it" wanted me to do.*
>
> —Shakti Gawain

The word *surrender* frightens some because it calls to mind losing a battle or spinelessness. But in interpersonal relationships, surrendering is simply acknowledging that sometimes the only thing I can change is *my* attitude, and that doing so has a profound effect on everything else. Making "surrender" your mantra is much shorter and to the point than saying to yourself, "Stop trying to dictate who comes into your life and what he'll be like and when he will call."

The basic principles of a Surrendered Single are that she:

- acknowledges her desire to attract and marry a man who's right for her;
- lets go of the idea of a perfect man;
- receives compliments, gifts, help, and dates graciously whenever possible;
- takes responsibility for and focuses on her own happiness and fulfillment;
- relinquishes control of the pace of the courtship;
- strives to be vulnerable;
- honors her desire to be married by ending dead-end relationships;

- checks for safety before she risks herself physically or emotionally.

A Surrendered Single is:

- open where she was guarded;
- optimistic where she was cynical;
- feminine where she was tough;
- gracious where once she fended for herself;
- respectful where she used to feel superior.

When a single woman surrenders, she doesn't try to manipulate a man to express his feelings, devotion, or commitment. She knows that would render his words meaningless. It creates the same kind of tension and frustration as when you twist someone's arm to do something rather than letting him decide when and how he wants to do it. She refrains from making ultimatums, nagging, criticizing, and correcting the man she is romantically involved with. She knows she can't improve someone else, and that trying to do so will cost her intimacy.

Instead of indulging in negative thinking about men and dating, she knows that there are both pleasures and risks involved in discovering an intimate relationship.

A Surrendered Single lets go of the negative beliefs she's been holding on to like a security blanket, such as:

- There are no good single men out there.
- I'm too old to attract someone.
- Dating is too much trouble.

At first surrendering will feel awkward and frightening. But so what? No one ever died from these feelings. They're trivial compared to the payoff.

## Take the Quiz: Are You Attracting the Man Who's Right for You?

Answer each question "rarely," "sometimes," or "frequently."

| DO YOU: | RARELY | SOMETIMES | FREQUENTLY |
|---|---|---|---|
| 1. *Date only men—even once—who meet your physical, financial, or educational standards?* | | | |
| 2. *Ask men out on dates if you're interested, just to get the ball rolling?* | | | |
| 3. *Believe you would attract the right man if you were prettier, younger, thinner, etc.?* | | | |
| 4. *Think marriage is too dangerous these days because so many people get divorced?* | | | |
| 5. *Find that your work, friendships, or hobbies are unfulfilling?* | | | |
| 6. *Stay in relationships whether or not they're headed toward marriage?* | | | |
| 7. *Secretly believe that you're smarter than the men you date?* | | | |
| 8. *Regret that you broke up or divorced a certain man or men?* | | | |
| 9. *Believe you have to sacrifice things you like when you get married?* | | | |
| 10. *Have sex with a man before he commits to you exclusively?* | | | |

| DO YOU: | RARELY | SOMETIMES | FREQUENTLY |
|---|---|---|---|
| 11. *Show affection for a man by doing helpful things for him, such as running his errands, cleaning his apartment, or writing his résumé?* | | | |
| 12. *Have a hard time finding a man you can trust?* | | | |
| 13. *Go for long periods without being approached by a man for a date?* | | | |
| 14. *Like to develop a friendship before you start dating someone?* | | | |
| 15. *Feel more confident in a work setting than you do in the dating arena?* | | | |
| 16. *Laugh with your friends at jokes about how immature or lazy men are?* | | | |
| 17. *Mistrust your intuition in picking a romantic partner because it's let you down so many times before?* | | | |
| 18. *Hear yourself dismissing compliments (i.e., "This dress is so old") or refusing gifts ("You shouldn't have! It's too expensive")?* | | | |
| 19. *Suspect good guys are boring?* | | | |
| 20. *Offer to pay your share on a date?* | | | |

## Quiz Scoring: Are You Attracting the Man Who's Right for You?

**To total your score, give yourself:**

- *5 points for each "rarely"*
- *3 points for each "sometimes"*
- *1 point for each "frequently"*

- *Add all three columns together for a final score (somewhere between 20 and 100).*

### 40 or Less: You're Standing in Your Own Way

You want to meet the man who's right for you, but you're unwittingly fending him off because you fear disappointment. You deserve to have a man who adores you and wants to make you happy, so help him get close to you by receiving graciously, making yourself available, practicing better self-care, and getting rid of the ex-boyfriends who are still cluttering up your dating space. Yes, you've had a broken heart or two, but you can leave your ivory tower and still protect yourself. You'll never get the relationship you crave any other way.

### 41 to 65: Are You Comfortable on That Fence?

You don't like to feel vulnerable, but you're not completely zipped up in armor, either. If you're unattached, men notice you and flirt with you, and that's when you really get nervous. Either the man who's right for you will need a good pair of running shoes or you could practice standing still. Consider accepting dates liberally and think of them as practice for the dating season.

If you're in a relationship, you may be sending out mixed messages that make him wonder if you'll stick around. Make a point to receive gifts and compliments graciously, express your desires, and listen to your intuition. Relax when you're tempted to take charge, and you'll stay out of trouble. Surrendering really will help you find the relationship you always dreamed you would have.

### 66 or Above: It Won't Be Long

You have an attractive, feminine style that men recognize and respond to immediately. Either you're already in a relationship with a great guy, or you'll meet him by the time you finish reading this paragraph. You're willing to risk your heart, but you're putting the odds in your favor by setting your limits and letting him take the lead. There's nothing to stop you from having a passionate, intimate romance.

# Surrendering Changes You Little by Little

*The big things that come our way are . . . the fruit of seeds planted in the daily routine of our work.*

—William Feather

No trumpets sound on the day you surrender. In fact, it doesn't happen on a single day, but over time.

When Fiona first came to a Surrendered Singles group, she wasn't convinced that control was her issue. "I just haven't met the right guy yet," she said. "I think it's because Southern California is just so superficial." Still, she agreed to try a couple Surrendered techniques like smiling at everyone she saw and being open to accepting dates because, she admitted, doing things her way had left her feeling alone, tired, and defensive.

She also told us about a flirtation at work. "He's really attractive, but not a possibility because he's too young and he smokes." Yet Fiona agreed that the flirtation made her feel feminine and tingly, so she decided to continue without trying to force anything. In the meantime, she announced to friends that she was available for blind dates and joined an Internet dating service. Before long she went from not dating at all to dating once or twice a week.

"I'm surprised to find that I'm enjoying it," she remarked. "I thought it was so much work, but when I focus on receiving and don't try to control anything, it's more relaxing and enjoyable. I still get nervous and scared, but I'm also excited."

On one date, Fiona felt herself wanting to reach for the bill so he wouldn't think she was cheap, but she resisted. Her date seemed happy to pay for both of them, and for the first time Fiona realized not only that she could receive graciously, but that she liked being treated!

She survived that experience, so she decided to experiment with surrendering control of the conversation by being quiet so she could listen to her own heart—and her date's—rather than trying to perform by thinking of something clever to say next. Instead of one lull after another, she found her dates were happy to entertain her and lead the conversation.

Meanwhile, she learned about herself and about them.

Fiona found the courage to override her cynicism and let the men who wanted to woo her have a chance. (Granted, it wasn't easy.) She reminded herself that she wanted an intimate relationship more than she wanted to assuage her fear by staying in control.

Slowly but surely, Fiona was changing. She looked softer and more attractive. She felt more feminine and more open. "I was single before because I was afraid of the alternative," she admitted, "not because I hadn't met the right guy."

Ultimately, there was no reason to complain about the lack of available men. They were everywhere.

Not coincidentally, Scott—the younger man at work—asked flirtatious Fiona out on a date. Perhaps he noticed she was less guarded or that she seemed more confident in the wake of so many men pursuing her. In any case, she was surrendering to the idea that she couldn't possibly know if she would like someone unless she went out with him, so she said yes.

By now, Fiona knew better than to suggest a place and time to meet or do the back-and-forthing that would make their schedules mesh.

She didn't try to keep him interested with sex.

She didn't try to find out if he was interested in a commitment or just a summer romance.

Fiona stayed in the moment. He pursued her with home-cooked meals, adventurous dates, and experiments in what would please her. Scott arranged their dates and paid for them. Fiona enjoyed herself and accepted a second date, then a third.

How normal. What bliss.

Other offers for dates were still coming in, and although Fiona was mostly interested in Scott, she accepted them to keep her options open, knowing that she couldn't predict whether Scott would decide to take things to the next level. "I would fret because he didn't e-mail me for one day, but I sat on my hands and didn't try to draw out a message by sending him one first. I didn't want to cheat myself out of being pursued, so I just waited to receive what he had to offer. For me, being the aggressor was about controlling so that I wouldn't feel vulnerable, but I don't need to do that anymore."

After only three months of surrendering and a few weeks of dating, Scott told Fiona that he wanted to see only her. Thrilled, Fiona agreed that she didn't want to see anyone else either.

Each of the small steps that Fiona took eventually brought her to where she always wanted to be: with a wonderful man who adored her.

## Will Reading This Book Make Me Seem Desperate?

There's nothing more humiliating for a single woman than feeling desperate—or imagining that other people see her that way.

Reading this book is not going to make you seem anxious, needy, or quick to take the first man who comes along. When you start dating, you *will* feel transparent, as if everyone around you can see your insecurities and is judging you for them. That's simply part of the vulnerability of dating. In reality, however, people aren't really paying attention to your insecurities; they're not thinking about us as much as we imagine. And if they *are* thinking about you, nobody will think less of you for receiving offers and dates from the men you meet. Acknowledging that you want a romantic partner is not desperate—it's honest and brave. Good people will find your vulnerability endearing and empathize with your desires.

Desperation is feeling that you have to find someone immediately, no matter what the cost. Desperation drives you to be sexual long before you would normally be comfortable and settle for unacceptable men. It prompts you to reveal too much too soon, which leaves you with little power and lots of risk.

Surrendering, on the other hand, means honoring your desires and protecting yourself from overinvesting. Rather than taking the first guy who comes along or rejecting everybody out of fear, you'll be able to make well-informed decisions based on your desires.

Finally, taking time for yourself is a fundamental part of surrendering. Long walks, dinners with your girlfriends, journal writing—or just cuddling up on the couch with a book or a romantic movie helps you to hear your own heart. When you do, urgency and desperation are replaced with confidence.

Surrendering will not humiliate you; on the contrary, it will make you strong and surefooted on the road to attracting the right man.

## Seek Out a Wife Who Has the Kind of Relationship You Desire

*The healthy and strong individual is the one who asks for help when he needs it. Whether he's got an abscess on his knee or in his soul.*

—Rona Barrett

As rewarding as it is, surrendering isn't always easy. Neither is dating. So it's important to have someone who has been down the same road guide your passage.

Happily married women are a wonderful resource, and I suggest that you seek one out to be your mentor in attracting the man who's right for you. If someone in your immediate circle of friends and family fits that description, ask her for input, support, and advice. If you know two such women, talk to them both.

If you don't know anyone who has the kind of marriage you would like to have, then think of people who are just outside your circle. Does your coworker or your friend's sister have a happy union? How about someone on your softball team or in your professional organization who is clearly in love with her husband? Somewhere around you is a woman who has what you're seeking. Most likely, if you approach her graciously, she will happily tell you what she knows. That's the power of sisterhood.

Most people like the feeling of helping someone, so chances are, your married mentor will be glad to help you. Everyone loves to watch the miracle of a romance unfold, so she'll enjoy talking to you as much as you'll benefit from talking to her. She'll probably feel honored that you want her advice.

Think of your mentor as someone who can help you make difficult decisions, calm your fears, and reflect back to you what she hears in your own heart. Call her whenever you're feeling uncertain, obsessed, terrified, nervous, or curious about something related to dating.

## KEEP YOUR EYES ON YOUR OWN PAPER

When you're craving an intimate relationship, it's tempting to focus on someone outside of yourself. Does he like me? Will he ask me out? Was he flirting? Does he love me? Will we get married? The more important questions to ask yourself, however, are: Do I like him? Would I go out with him? Do I want to flirt? Do I love him? Would I marry him?

Like children who look at their classmates' papers to see who's coloring in the lines, we sometimes look to a man expecting to find information that will help us make decisions about our own lives. When it comes to matters of the heart, though, the most valuable information will come from inside you.

## SURRENDERING BRINGS OUT YOUR BEST SELF

Surrendering isn't about being so desperate you'll go out with just anyone. It will not make you into a Scarlett O'Hara or Barbie.

It certainly won't make you a milquetoast.

Rather, a Surrendered Single takes the focus off things outside of her and looks inward. She honors her desire to have a romantic partner by finding the courage to risk her heart, but no more than necessary. In doing so, she builds on her best qualities and gains confidence and virtue.

She strives for balance between work and play, finding satisfaction in her career, pursuing hobbies, and enjoying friendships. Those efforts bring her contentment, which in turn makes her more attractive and inviting to the right man.

She becomes the best version of herself.

# 1 SURRENDER TO YOUR DESIRE TO BE HAPPILY MARRIED

*What's terrible is to pretend that the second-rate is first-rate. To pretend that you don't need love when you do.*

—DORIS LESSING

*Dishonoring your desire to get married is a way of protecting yourself from disappointment and trying to avoid becoming dependent.*

*If you've been denying—on any level—that you want to get married, it's time to stop living in fear and start acknowledging your true desires, both to yourself and to others. Following your natural longings is nothing to be embarrassed about, and denying them can keep even a smart, independent woman from getting what she wants most.*

*Tell your friends and family. Say, "I want to get married to a great guy someday," or "I'm looking forward to sharing my life with someone." If you can't say it to anyone else yet, at least say it to yourself.*

*Denying what you want is a way of controlling your desires so that you can ward off the fear, disappointment, and humiliation. Ultimately, however, such denial and control will stand between you and finding the love you crave.*

*Surrender to your desire to be married and you give that desire the chance to become a reality.*

## Who Needs a Husband?

That was the question *Time* magazine posed on a cover a few years ago. "More women are saying no to marriage and embracing the single life," the cover line read. "Are they happy?"

Some women are comfortable living solo and don't want to get married. However, if you're not one of them, pretending that you are will ultimately render you heartbroken and unhappy.

When I was dating, I told myself that I didn't *want* to get married. The dialogue between me and myself was an elaborate way of avoiding my fear of divorce. Yet my loneliness and desire for a partner were acute. I wasn't so much "embracing the single life" as I was trying to avoid future pain.

My situation was not unusual. Phrases like "embracing the single life" are very often shorthand for "avoiding the risk of a disappointment." Sometimes the women in my workshops will say, "I'm pretty happy being single. I'm not lonely or anything." But if that were true, why would they take my workshop?

Sure, it feels less vulnerable to say that you're completely content being single. You may think the take-charge thing to do when you haven't met the right man is to act like you're not interested in men because you're so fulfilled in your career or busy with ski trips and school.

Admitting there's a hole in your heart exposes you. We all want to be perceived as independent and strong. When we admit loneliness, we fear that people will think we're less self-sufficient—or, even worse, that they'll feel sorry for us.

## Lying to Yourself Is a Form of Control

*N*ot taking that risk is a way of trying to stay in control. Ironically, denying what you really want so you can avoid possible hurt puts you even further away from getting what you want and more in the face of the pain.

Admitting that I craved a wonderful man and surrendering to that desire put me at risk of heartbreak. It was also the critical first step of embarking on what has turned out to be a remarkable love story that has lasted more than twelve years and seems very likely to last a lifetime.

## Let People Who Love You Help You Look

> *You probably wouldn't worry about what people think of you if you could know how seldom they do.*
>
> —Olin Miller

I'm not suggesting that you put your life on hold until you meet someone or that you announce your matrimonial ambitions on a first date. In fact, doing so is yet another form of control. What I'm adamant about is that you tell yourself the truth: You desire someone who will treasure, love, protect, admire, and adore you.

If you're nervous about telling yourself the truth, perhaps you subscribe to one of the following myths:

*Myth:* "If I admit I'm lonely, even to myself, I'll seem desperate."
*Reality:* Loneliness and desperation are different. Loneliness says, "I'd like to be with someone else. I crave companionship, romance, and intimacy." Desperation says, "I can't stand being alone and my self-respect is low. I will take anyone, even if I know he's not right for me." Loneliness is not undignified. It's a natural human emotion that we all feel at times.

*Myth:* "If I admit to others that I want to get married, people will think I'm not serious about my career."
*Reality:* Even if other people are thinking about you that much, they aren't likely to think you have to choose either career or marriage. Having the desire to get married doesn't wipe out your accomplishments and ambition; the two are not mutually exclusive. Everyone knows there are many very successful married women out there. No one will be surprised to learn that you want both a fulfilling career and a passionate romance.

*Myth:* "If I admit I want to get married, people will think I'm undesirable if I don't get married soon."
*Reality:* Again, it's hard to imagine someone having enough free time to think about your love life so much, but just for the sake of argument, imagine a friend says to you, "I want to get married." Would your next assumption be that there's something terribly wrong with her because she's still not marred six months later? Of course not. Truth is, "You *can't* hurry love." We all know it takes time. Good people will think you're brave for telling the truth.

*Myth:* "If I admit that I'm lonely, I'll scare off the kind of man I want to meet."

> ***Reality:*** If you were desperate and willing to settle for anyone, that might be true. But you'll still have your standards, and you won't have to settle for anybody who isn't just right for you. Acknowledging the vacancy in your life—the same way you would admit that you're looking for a job when you're unemployed—opens the door for that desire to become a reality.

In fact, there are some similarities between the way you approach finding love and the way you would look for a job. When you want a new job, you admit it. You network. People give you leads. You follow up on every one. You leave the dead ends behind, always cordially, and don't look back.

Another similarity is that when you're in the job market, the people who matter to you don't think you're weak or lacking simply because you need a job. Instead, they keep their ears and eyes open so they can help you find what you want. If you admit to your friends and family that you're in the market for the right man, they can not only encourage and support you, but also invite you to baseball games and parties where you're likely to meet someone.

There are, however, some differences between attracting romance and finding a job. One is that while you sometimes have to settle for a job because there are creditors at the door, you never have to settle for a husband. Another is that you don't have to aggressively hunt for a husband the way you would your dream position, because he will find you.

## Romantic Love Is Your Birthright

> *If it is your time, love will track you down*
> *like a cruise missile.*
>
> —Lynda Barry

Some of us were told growing up that we shouldn't wait for Prince Charming and that we should be self-sufficient. You may have seen the bumper sticker that reads A WOMAN NEEDS A MAN LIKE A FISH NEEDS A BICYCLE. Maybe you've felt pressure to "embrace the single life" when really you just wish you could be happily married.

If you've been open about your desire to find the man who's right for you, maybe people have discouraged you by saying, "It never happens when you're looking for it," or "Don't want it so much." They may have meant well, but not only are they maddening to the single woman who is honest about what she wants, they're also confusing desire with desperation.

Saying that you don't want what you want is not helpful.

Your prince may not ride up on a white horse, but it's not too much to ask to spend your life with someone attractive who makes you feel like a princess. Being loved by a man is your birthright as a woman. Mating is one of the oldest, ingrained human instincts. While self-sufficiency is admirable, it doesn't fulfill your need to be held and touched, to be intimate with a man. Acting as though you don't crave a leading man in your life doesn't make it so, but it does contribute to keeping you single.

## The Look of Love Is Congruent

Once you've acknowledged that you want to be married, you'll change inside. You'll feel more relaxed, because your thoughts and your feelings will be aligned. You'll feel the relief that comes with baring a secret that's been eating at you.

Consequently, you'll change on the outside, too. When you're in denial about wanting to be married, it shows on your face—in the way you wrinkle your forehead or shift your eyes when someone looks directly into them. It's in the way you walk and hunch your shoulders. Your defenses show like a coat of armor.

When you surrender to the desire to be married—when you embrace it—your countenance and body will change. Your eyes won't dart. Instead, you will see possibilities, and you will smile with your eyes. Your body language will be different. Instead of wearing "I don't need a man" body armor, you'll signal "I'm available to the right guy."

If you've ever seen someone smile when they're angry, you know how strange someone looks when they're incongruent. They send mixed signals that make them hard to read and uncomfortable to be around. The only way to be congruent is to honor and to express your feelings instead of trying to dismiss them. As soon as you do, everyone else will unconsciously pick up on that. That gives potential suitors the encouragement they need to approach you or invite you to spend time with them. A man you will absolutely love is much more likely to spot you if he sees that you're available.

And once he spots you, there's a very good chance that you'll never even think of embracing the single life again.

# 2
# GIVE UP THE IDEA OF THE PERFECT MAN

*One who looks for a friend without faults will have none.*

—Hasidic saying

***Do you size up every man you meet against a mental checklist? Do you have requirements regarding age, education, income, previous marital status, background?***

***It's time to surrender your checklist and accept an imperfect man.***

***You can be blissfully happy with an imperfect man. You will certainly be perpetually lonely without one.***

## YOUR STANDARDS MAY BE TOO HIGH TO LEAP IN A SINGLE BOUND

Maybe the man of your dreams has green eyes, curly dark hair, and towers over you. Perhaps he's a successful businessman with a private airplane, or a family man who wants to live on a ranch. You may meet someone who fills your bill exactly.

More likely, your beau will touch your heart and impress your mind, but in some ways he won't be quite what you expected. That means you won't necessarily recognize him when you first see him, especially if your search is limited to someone who meets all the criteria on your list.

If you approach dating with a mental checklist, you might pass up the cute guy who works at the bookstore because he doesn't seem upwardly mobile enough. You would have to turn down the friend of a friend because you've heard he's a slob. You would decline dinner with a coworker because you've sworn off office relationships. Now you and your checklist are staying home on Friday night because nobody made a high enough grade to date you.

Or maybe you'll go out with practically anybody once, then decide to stop seeing him because he slurped his soup, kept every piece of junk in his garage, or was three years younger than you.

If you find you're breaking off budding relationships, not dating at all, or just generally dissatisfied with the available pool of men, you are waiting for a perfect man.

Make a list of all the available men you know and those people whom you have dated. Why have you chosen not to go out with the single men in your circle? Have you discouraged a friend from fixing you up with someone she thinks you might like? Who decided to end the relationships you've had? Why did you decline a second date?

Write down your answers to these questions. See if you find patterns that reveal the ways in which perfectionism made you pass up good men.

## A Checklist Is a Suit of Armor

> *The great soul surrenders itself to fate.*
>
> —Lucius Anneaus Seneca

As we all know, no one is perfect.

There is no such thing as the perfect man. So if you're holding out for the perfect man, you're actually avoiding intimacy—probably because you're afraid—even if you don't realize it.

A checklist is a suit of armor that protects you from having to face your fears, even if you are dating and saying you want to share your life. Maybe you suffered a painful breakup or divorce, so you're afraid to go through that again. Maybe your first boyfriend died unexpectedly in a car crash, so you can't bear the thought of being left alone again. Perhaps you are tenderhearted and feel that you just aren't up for risking the potential pain of giving your soul and not getting the same in return. The sting of heartbreak leaves a stubborn imprint and tempts us to try to control our lives to protect against it ever happening again.

By holding on to the qualities you want in a man, you are setting up an unrealistic expectation. As long as it's never met—and it won't be—you don't have to risk your heart. Keeping your checklist is a way to stay invulnerable.

* * *

Surrendering means acknowledging that you can't exert control by dictating the qualities of an acceptable future mate and still find the love you crave. It requires changing your attitude toward the men around you instead of complaining about your circumstances.

Whatever the reason for your fear, it's important to face it. Your fear is keeping you lonely, and your checklist is allowing you to hold on to your fear. Until you're willing to walk past that apprehension—even if your heart is pounding and your palms are sweating—you will never experience a man's total adoration of you. You'll never experience the emotional connection, companionship, and physical passion of a committed relationship unless you're willing to look an imperfect man in the eye, feel that fear, and keep going.

That's exactly what this book will show you how to do.

## Finding Out If You're Lovable

> *Love is an irresistible desire to be irresistibly desired.*
>
> —Robert Frost

Have you ever had a girlfriend who seemed to avoid men and then complained that she never met anyone? On some level she was afraid. For such a woman, it's second nature to make a list of the things she doesn't like about a potential partner. He has a paunch. He never wants to discuss his feelings. He won't tell his mother he's too busy to help her. He did drugs ten years ago.

Diana thought she was open to all kinds of men and completely available until she started ticking off the reasons she wouldn't date men—even once. "One lived too far, another was too young, another had a five-year-old, another came on too strong, another one—" She stopped abruptly.

As Diana was saying these things, she realized she had probably shut out some great guys, so she tried to explain: "I'm just trying to make sure I don't waste my time when nothing's going to come of it," she insisted. "It's so awful to get your hopes up about a guy you're not compatible with."

True enough. But you can't know that until you go out with him.

Although Diana thought she was just being practical, she realized that her true motivation was trying to avoid ever feeling disappointed again.

She made a decision on the spot to let go of her ideas about her perfect man. She stopped trying to control who would walk through her door. She surrendered to the possibilities.

Then a man who was both too young (forty-five to her fifty-two) and lived too far away (240 miles) contacted her through a dating service and asked her out. They clicked, and he told her how glad he was that Diana had responded to him this time.

"What do you mean, this time?" she asked.

"Last time I contacted you, I never got a response. But I decided to try again, and this time you responded," he replied.

Being willing to accept a less-than-perfect man doesn't mean you're going to commit to just anybody. It's fair to know that there are things that you absolutely can't tolerate in a potential mate. You *should* have standards. For instance, if your children are raised and you're not willing to be a mother to young children again, then it's fair to eliminate men with custody of their small children as potential dates.

But sometimes standards are a façade for a ridiculous screening process that's meant to protect you from having to open up to a man. Then those so-called standards keep you alone.

When you're finding something wrong with *every* guy, there's a very good chance it's because you're afraid you'll never reach that point where your lover knows you completely and still finds you absolutely desirable. You're afraid that you're not lovable.

Each of us wonders whether there's someone in the world who will actually put up with us and commit to us for life. Diana, who knew she wanted to have a husband someday, was especially afraid of dating younger men because her last boyfriend had made it clear he would never marry someone her age. Since there was nothing she could do about that, she felt that she was destined for rejection, especially from younger men. She worried that she would get involved and attached, only to be let down again.

No matter how certain you are that no man could love you if he really knew you, you are no different than every married person who once feared the same thing. The wonderful thing about a romance is that even the most dejected parts of us begin to heal in the warmth of adoration and cherishing from someone who is absolutely crazy about us despite all our quirks. The incredible thing about falling in love is that your lover thoroughly adores you—yes, even you, especially you—exactly the way you are.

Despite the wounds from her last relationship, Diana found the courage and strength to date men who seemed interested, even if they were younger. "After all," she explained, "how do I know how old my true love will be?"

## No Neon Sign Will Point to the One

Until you go out with a man a few times, you won't know if you're going to enjoy his company or be impressed by his mind. Nor can you possibly know if he's somebody you can trust. Before you commit to him, you have no idea what it's like to be in an exclusive, intimate relationship with him.

We all wish we could know instantly whether a man is going to be *the* one, break our hearts, bring out the best in us, be hopelessly unfaithful, or make us laugh well into old age. We'd like to be able to look at him and just know. Or at least be certain by the end of the first date if he's *it*.

If we could tell right away, it would take a lot of the fear (and excitement) out of dating. We could proceed only after we knew we weren't going to get dropped. The trouble is, you can't know.

No neon sign will flash when your future husband passes you on the street.

That means it's necessary to risk our hearts at least a little in order to find out if a man in front of us is someone we could love madly.

This is no small thing for those of us who are scared of being abandoned or rejected. I know this because I too was terrified when I was dating. Out of fear, I dismissed men. I looked hard for "reasons" to stop seeing the man who would later be my husband. I remember finding fault with him for sending me a thank-you note after I'd made him brunch. I said as much in front of Candace, my best friend.

"That's kind of wimpy that he sent me a thank-you note, isn't it?" I said warily. And, on some level, I also thought he must be desperate. Only a desperate, overly polite mama's boy would send a thank-you note.

"Wimpy?" she responded incredulously. "No, it's not wimpy. It's very sweet."

Sweet. Right.

I wasn't used to sweet so it made me uncomfortable.

Luckily, despite my terror and my suspicions, I knew Candace was right. I took a deep breath and reframed my perception of the card, borrowing her wise perspective. It worked. I didn't blow him off when he asked me out again. I kept agreeing to see him. Eventually I realized that there was nothing hopeless about this man.

Finally, what I feared most came to pass. He saw me with bed-hair, endured my worst PMS, and learned that I viewed check bouncing as a normal part of cash-flow management.

I not only survived after exposing my soft underbelly to this man, I gained the sweet acceptance and adoration I'd craved. I learned that the only way to have the thing I most wanted and feared was to stay the course—to keep seeing him, despite my pounding heart and shallow breathing.

## Get in the Habit of Hanging In There

If you're like me, you'll find yourself wanting to run away from promising relationships and thinking of dozens of "logical" justifications for why you should.

However, if you make yourself stay, the rewards will be great. Most important, even if you date a few men who really aren't right for you, you will start to build the muscles that give you the strength and perspective you'll need to keep auditioning men.

Ultimately, the training will pay off: You will attract a man who, though he isn't perfect, will be right for you. This won't just be anybody who loves the real you—this will also be somebody with whom you are also impressed.

Of course, none of that will happen unless you decide to hang in there even if he talks with his mouth full, hasn't balanced his checkbook in three years or—God forbid—sends you a thank-you note.

## Crumple Up Your Checklist

Making a commitment to stay the course in a relationship despite minor irritations is frightening. It means there's no valid excuse to stop you from committing to an imperfect man who's perfect for you.

But it can be tricky, too. How do we know which imperfections to overlook and which to run from?

Now that I've watched thousands of wives transform lonely marriages into happy, intimate relationships, it's obvious which problems are insurmountable and which are just part of life's little irritations. There are certain types of men you'll want to avoid committing to: practicing addicts, physical abusers, and men who can't be faithful. For now, crumple up that checklist and throw it away. As it turns out, what makes a man a "good guy" has absolutely nothing to do with whether he works in a law firm or drives a tractor.

Contented couples know this already. They also understand that if they had married someone else, they would have had a different set of problems. They remember vividly the moment they realized they were two of the same kind. They call it falling in love.

In other words, feelings of attraction, and the love and romance that follow, are beacons for helping us find someone we match. This person will not be perfect, of course, because no one is. He will, however, have some fantastic, interesting qualities and characteristics that balance well with yours. You can either lament about what attributes he doesn't have or celebrate the ones he does.

Surrendering means accepting all of his qualities, and trying to improve only yourself.

Just as he may have to accept that you talk to your mother every day, exaggerate from time to time, or rarely arrive somewhere promptly, you too will have to make concessions.

Having confidence that someone who knows you inside and out loves you anyway will more than compensate for those small irritations.

There is an imperfect man who is perfect for you, too.

# 3

# STOP MALE-BASHING AND START ADMIRING MEN

*What we anticipate seldom occurs; what we least expected generally happens.*

—Benjamin Disraeli

*We tend to believe what we hear ourselves saying.*

*If you're in the habit of putting down men or telling mean jokes about them when you talk with your friends, it's time to find a new hobby.*

*If you talk about how unpleasant men are, you will start to believe it. This is counterproductive to your efforts to attract the man who is right for you.*

*Surrender to the notion that a man has qualities you lack—and lacks qualities you have—simply because he is a man. Switch to the mantra "I love men."*

## Watch What You Tell Yourself About Men

Sure, it's fun to kid about how the difference between savings bonds and men is that bonds mature, but if you want someone with whom you can share your life, you can't afford to partake in conversations that degrade men. Even in jest, they affect your thinking. They subtly influence your attitude about the group at the butt of the joke.

For instance, let's say that you fear that all men are cheaters and you get an e-mail joke about a man who was cheating on his wife, which you then repeat to some coworkers. You are reinforcing a negative and unfounded belief about men. Some men are cheaters, but most are not, and lumping the good ones in with the creeps is offensive and unfair.

I gained a new insight into this after I'd been married for several years. Previously, I was quite a male-basher. If John bristled at a Post-it note printed with "Men have only two faults: everything they say and everything they do," a beer commercial that portrayed men as incompetent idiots, or a greeting card that said men are scum, I'd tell him to lighten up.

After I started acting with (and feeling) more respect toward him, the same comments that were offensive to him offended me, too. They were making fun of *my* husband! They were hurting the man who loved me, the person who wanted the best for me. For the first time, I felt the sting of the potshots.

For instance, John brings a refreshing playfulness and sense of fun to our relationship, even at the most stressful times. The savings bond joke makes the point that men are immature. I used to think of my husband as immature, because when I was trying to be very serious and worry about our future, he would put socks on his hands as puppets and have the sock puppets tell me to relax. Now I call his playfulness entertaining and reassuring.

See how the same qualities you might consider negative can be reframed as assets? Since you choose the lens through which you view male behavior, begin by taking off your dark glasses.

## Putting Men Down Doesn't Make Us Feel Better

*Happiness is a function of accepting what is.*

—Werner Erhard

If we convince ourselves that men are inconsiderate and unfaithful, we reason that we're really not missing much. Interestingly, this line of thinking doesn't quell our desire for romance and companionship.

If it did, you wouldn't be reading this book.

If you find yourself with girlfriends in the midst of a barrage of critical anti-men humor, you might be tempted to go with the flow. But you can just as easily put a new topic on the table by throwing out questions like, "What's the best date you've ever been on?" or "When you were little, did you want to get married and have kids?" After all, if you're going to participate in the conversation, there's nothing that says you can't nudge it in a direction you prefer.

Wallowing in cynicism affects the kinds of signals you send out to men. If you habitually make critical comments and roll your eyes at their behavior, you'll give men the impression that you don't hold them in high esteem. If you've spent your time and energy programming yourself to see them as contemptible, they'll pick up on that. Far from finding you alluring and approachable, men more likely will keep their distance—and find someone who does appreciate them.

## Men Will Never Be Good Women

We all have our moments when we wonder why men can't be more empathetic or communicative. You might get frustrated because you feel like you never know what he's thinking or feeling. He certainly won't tell you in the same way that a girlfriend would.

When we complain about the way men communicate, what we're really saying is, "Why can't men be more like women?"

Men can't ever be good women—and for this we can be glad.

Perhaps they are not as expressive as your girlfriends, but men do communicate in their own way. Rather than trying to control them by drawing them out, a much more gratifying approach is to leave lots of wide-open spaces in the conversation. Don't rush their words or preempt their ideas. That's when you'll hear their heart messages loud and clear.

If your man still doesn't talk enough to satisfy your conversational appetite, you're not unusual. That's why girlfriends are so vital. They keep us from relying on one person to meet all of our emotional needs.

It's easy to forget that men come from a different culture. In the male culture, talking about feelings is not a common or comfortable practice. Neither is talking on the phone. Or talking as much as women talk, for that matter. According to author Deborah Tannen, "saying that men talk about baseball in order to avoid talking about their feelings is the same as saying that women talk about their feelings in order to avoid talking about baseball." Clearly, men connect to others in ways completely different from women, and the only sane thing to do about it is to surrender to the differences by accepting and appreciating them.

## Use Manners in the Male Culture

*Don't flatter yourself that friendship authorizes you*
*to say disagreeable things to your intimates.*
*The nearer you come into relation with a person,*
*the more necessary do tact and courtesy become.*

—Oliver Wendell Holmes, Jr.

Elena was always trying to get her boyfriend, Ben, to open up about his feelings. She once urged him to talk about his disappointment when he was passed over for a promotion. Another time, she asked him how he had felt—really felt—when he went through his divorce. But Ben didn't want to talk about these sore topics, so he responded to her interrogations with vague shrugs and grunts.

On one level, of course, Elena wanted to understand Ben, and knowing about how he reacted to missing out on a promotion and getting divorced would be telling. On another level, however, Elena was looking for reassurance from Ben that he loved her and trusted her with his secrets. Those aren't questions you can force answers to. Her prodding was a roundabout—and controlling—attempt to get him to say what she was longing to hear.

When Ben didn't volunteer his feelings as much as Elena thought he should, she tried to "help" him open up by telling him it wasn't healthy to keep his feelings inside. The more she pushed, the more irritated and defensive Ben became. She couldn't understand why this was irritating to him, so she discussed it with her girlfriends, who all agreed that since he obviously wasn't emotionally available, he would never make her happy.

Granted, you want to be with a man who will talk to you about more than baseball. However, trying to control him by dragging him into a conversation about his emotions will not do the trick. Good listeners learn a lot more than amateur therapists. Men like them better, too. And you'll preserve the intimacy, to boot.

For instance, Ben did tell Elena once that he loved having custody of his kids on a part-time basis. "I'm always so happy to see them," he confided, "and then I'm always so happy to see them go, so I can have a break. I think it's a great setup."

True, Ben's satisfaction with his custody arrangements didn't have anything to do with his relationship with Elena, which is what she most wanted to know about. It did reveal his devotion as a father, through his ability to see the good in his situation and an appealing frankness. Ben also showed his feelings by putting his arm around Elena and kissing her, actions which are more significant than any words.

"How do you feel?" is an awkward question for men. It is the equivalent of asking a woman how much she weighs. Think of the male culture the way you would any foreign culture—not bad, just different. Just because you don't share those customs doesn't make them wrong and your "customs" right.

This is not to say that a man will never tell you how he feels—

he will from time to time, as part of normal conversation. The key is not to put him on the spot about it. Recognize that you can have a great emotional connection with him simply by laughing together, hugging, sharing *your* feelings, and accepting his gifts.

Expecting a man to be intimate with you the same way a girlfriend would be—by sharing feelings and processing them endlessly—is as unfair as it is unrealistic.

Instead of asking your date how he feels as a litmus test for his capacity for intimacy, ask yourself how *you* feel when you're around him. Had Elena asked herself this question, she might have answered, "Happy, except when we fight because he won't open up to me."

Surrendering means that instead of using a crowbar on the conversation, you listen carefully to what your date volunteers. That's where you'll find out how he liked the movie, what he hopes to accomplish in life, what he thinks about marriage and, perhaps most important, how he likes you.

# 4 FLIRT WITH EVERY MAN YOU SEE

> *Never frown, because you never know*
> *who might be falling in love with your smile.*
> —Justine Milton

*To find a man you absolutely love, you're going to have to face your fears and find the courage to start attracting dates now—not after the holiday, not when you lose some weight, not when the kids grow up, or when you get a new job. None of that matters anyway, but your attitude does.*

*It's time to master the art of flirting. Almost every romantic encounter in the world starts with an exchange of smiles, so it's important to have yours at the ready at all times. Start by smiling at every man you see, whether you encounter him every day or he's a stranger. Smile at the guy chatting on his cell phone at your coffee stop, the man standing in line at the post office, the coworker in the next cubicle.*

*Give your sincere thanks or a compliment to at least one man every day, whether it's thanking him for his contribution to a project at work, complimenting his suit, or simply appreciating the box boy who helps you get the groceries out to the car.*

## Every Romance Starts with a Smile

You don't have to find the man you want to marry, because he will find you. In fact, he's already looking.

However, you do need to help him discover you. One of the surest ways to lead him to you is to smile when you see him. If you want to greet your husband-to-be with a smile the very first time you meet him, then it's important that you smile at all men. You don't yet know who is going to be the lucky guy!

Therefore, starting right now, give everybody you see—young or old—your best smile. Before you start thinking that this sounds crazy, let me tell you about a friend who didn't want anyone to think she was a ditz, easy, desperate, or that she was so unimportant as to actually have time for conversing with strangers. Most of all, though, she didn't like the unexpected or letting people know that she was vulnerable. She wanted always to appear in control.

One day when her life seemed to be at a low point (her best friend had moved away, she was about to be laid off, and she was in a going-nowhere relationship), she walked into her local library. There she saw a man not exactly her type who was leaning back in his chair, clearly bored by the work on his laptop.

He caught her eye and smiled, and in a split second she forgot how sorry she felt for herself and all the reasons she never smiled at anyone. She smiled back. He smiled bigger. For the rest of the afternoon my friend dutifully continued her research, getting up from time to time to check out books, go to the bathroom, and . . . well, walk past his desk to smile.

By the middle of the afternoon, they were dancing the dance of a wonderful flirtation, and just before closing, he came over to introduce himself. By the time they walked to the parking lot, they'd already made plans to get together the next day.

They haven't been apart since.

Not bad for a day's worth of smiles.

## Why You Should Be Friendly to Strangers

*What we anticipate seldom occurs; what we least expected generally happens.*

—Benjamin Disraeli

If the smiling idea still makes you a little nervous, that's fine. A lot of us were taught not to make eye contact with strangers. Perhaps other women have criticized you for being a flirt, or you fear that smiling indiscriminately will make you seem desperate. We tell ourselves not to give anybody the wrong idea. Most likely, though, we know that smiling can lead to the unexpected, and the unexpected often makes us feel as if we are out of control, and that makes us nervous.

None of these reasons, however, needs to stand between you and inviting a man to approach you with a smile. Here's why:

***Myth #1: "You shouldn't be friendly with a stranger."*** You're a grown woman; it's children, whose judgment is undeveloped, who shouldn't get too friendly with strangers. For you, it's fine. You're big enough now to tell people to go away when they're bothering you and to know whether it's okay to get into a car with somebody. You now have an adult with you to protect you at all times—yourself.

***Myth #2: "No one respects a flirtatious woman."*** One woman wondered if she needed to start feigning helplessness and batting her eyelashes à la Scarlett O'Hara to attract men. We've all seen women who are so over the top in their flirtatiousness that we shudder for all womankind. A simple smile, though, is neither pandering nor belittling. You needn't be sugary sweet nor sexual when you smile. You can just smile—nothing more. It is simply a signal that says you're open and friendly. Be yourself, but be your friendliest self.

***Myth #3: "When you smile at a man, he gets the wrong idea."*** A smile can mean many things. It can be nothing more than a friendly greeting, an acknowledgment that you've noticed someone who's noticed you—an end in itself. It can be an invitation for a conversation. A smile is a way to show approval or pleasure. Smiling at someone, however, is not a promise.

***Myth #4: "When you smile at a man, you're out of control; you don't know how he'll respond or what will follow."*** Okay, so this one isn't a myth. It's true that a smile may cause a man to approach you or talk to you, and you may not want to talk to every man you see. You don't have to. You can simply end the conversations that don't interest you but linger for the ones that do. The point is to cast a wide net.

The benefit of smiling at everyone you see is that you're communicating in a subtle yet visible way that you are clearly in the market. My friend Candace used to call this "sending out your scent." Think of cultures where single women wear a flower behind the left ear to signal their availability. Smile pretty and all who see you will know that you're ready to be pursued.

## Attention Without Intention

When I tell single women to start smiling at everyone they see, they balk at having to smile at men they already know they don't want to have anything to do with. The problem is, you can't tell in the first two seconds of an encounter (when you should be smiling) if a man is a good prospect or not.

Darcy realized she couldn't judge someone and smile at the same time. "It's hard for me to smile at men because I'm often too busy sizing them up," she said. "Is this guy a loony? Gay? Attached? Too old? Too young? Redneck? The list goes on and on. I'm not sure what I'm afraid will happen if they are any of those things. Most likely I'm trying to protect against getting myself into a situation that I can't control."

If you smile at a man you don't know, there's no telling what will happen. That means you won't be able to manage the situation or prepare a statement in case you're approached. So it isn't so much that he might be gay or stuck on his mother that holds us back from smiling—it's knowing that his initiating a conversation or flirting will remove us from our comfort zone.

You may find smiling at everyone you see challenging. You're not in the habit, or you may wonder if these people deserve your smile. But there are many benefits to smiling besides just opening yourself up so an attractive man can approach you.

One of the women in my workshop described consciously smiling at people as a confidence-building experience. Although she didn't feel she was good-looking, she threw back her shoulders and stood up straight when she smiled as she passed a man talking on his cell phone. The man pulled the phone away from his ear midsentence and said to her, "You're beautiful!"

Still another woman found that smiling gave her spirits a boost, as other people tended to respond in kind, giving her the impression that the world was full of friendly people. Of course, they were just mirroring her friendliness, but she experienced a greater sense of well-being and optimism.

The point is to make smiling a habit—an automatic response. In addition to building your confidence, flirting with every guy may also make you nervous, both because you're allowing yourself to be more open to meeting a man, and therefore more vulnerable, and because it's changing your routine. Any change—good, bad, or indifferent—is uncomfortable. Take it as a good sign if you feel nervous about the changes. Remember: If things are going to improve, they're going to have to change.

## You Can Put Your Foot Down

Flirting can also be scary because it seems like a slippery slope. It starts out innocently enough—let's say a man opens the door for you at a car repair shop and you smile at him—but it doesn't stop there. Next, he speaks to you, and you reply in kind, then he asks you out and you accept. Now you have to go out with him, and that's always nerve-racking, right?

But it's nerve-racking in a good way. And there are lots of points on that slippery slope where you could have put your foot down if you'd wanted to. You could have declined to talk to him. Or you could have turned down his offer to go out. That's always your choice. And smiling at him to begin with doesn't mean that you forfeit that choice. Just because you smile and flirt with somebody doesn't mean wedding bells are in the air. It may inspire a man to speak to you, but that's about it. After that the ball is back in your court, and it will go only as far as you want it to go.

A coworker once explained to me that you don't make a résumé to get a job. After all, nobody ever gets hired from just sending in a résumé. Instead, you make a résumé to get an interview, from which point you could get the job. Smiling is your résumé. Once you've gone on that first date, you can decide whether to go out with him again. Once you've dated him several times, you can decide if you'd like to commit to him.

Instead of thinking of flirting as a commitment, think of it as attention without intention. That's why it's perfectly acceptable to flirt with the elderly doorman and the butcher you would never want to see anywhere outside of the meat department. You're not signaling your intention when you flirt—just reaffirming your femininity and making every man around you feel like a million dollars.

## Flirt in a Skirt

Well, it doesn't have to be a skirt exactly, but clothing can be as flirtatious as a smile. It helps to wear something that shows off your female form. Think about it: Don't you move differently in skirts and dresses than you do in pants? You might not rush through the office, but walk a little more carefully. You're more aware of your legs and the movement of fabric in response to your body. Either consciously or unconsciously, you remind yourself that you're feminine, and feminine is what men are fundamentally attracted to. When you dress to flatter and show off that shape—no matter what age or size you are—a male admirer is sure to follow.

You do *not* have to be young or have a perfect figure to attract a man you will absolutely love, but you will want to flaunt whatever you've got.

That's not to say that you need to squeeze your womanly curves into a bikini. The point is to choose clothes that reveal your figure instead of hiding it. Pick a form-fitting top instead of a baggy sweatshirt. Choose jeans that hug your shape instead of oversized pants that hide it. Take off your coverup when you're sitting next to the pool. Most importantly, keep in mind that clothing that reveals your body is more appealing to men. Not only are they attracted to your shape, but such clothing expresses confidence, which is especially seductive.

In fact, the most important thing you can wear is an air of assurance.

It's also the most elusive.

One way to make sure that you feel as confident as possible is to put yourself together before you go out into the world. You'll *feel* more attractive if your hair and face are done and your clothes are attractive. You're likely to smile more easily and move more effortlessly. Also, men recognize that a woman who has invested time in her appearance wants to be admired, and they're more than happy to oblige, since admiring women is one of their favorite pastimes.

Of course, there will be times when you'll opt to "slum it" at the grocery store or decide not to wear makeup to the gym. You're only human. Still, you might consider putting on lipstick before you walk out the door, or wearing workout clothes that make you feel attractive instead of an old T-shirt and grungy sneakers. After all, you're going to be smiling at a lot of people and you could very well run into a handsome guy near the dairy case or on the next treadmill.

## Sincere Gratitude Is Flirtatious

> *Any fool can criticize, condemn, and complain—*
> *and most fools do.*
> —Dale Carnegie

There's one more thing that you can do to improve your outlook that will also make you more approachable: Express sincere gratitude to or compliment a man every single day.

Just as the woman who started smiling at everyone suddenly thought the world was a friendlier place, you'll be amazed at how generous and helpful everyone is when you start thanking at least one guy every day. This could be as simple as thanking the mail carrier for bringing your mail, appreciating the guy who puts together the monthly hikes for the local Sierra Club, or expressing gratitude to a presenter for making everything easy to understand.

If you're not in the habit of expressing gratitude to the people around you, you might have to take a hard look around to find somebody to appreciate every day. Once you start looking, though, you'll find plenty of opportunities. One woman thanked the audiovisual guy at a seminar by telling him how much she enjoyed the flashy presentation. "Oh, it was nothing," he said, shrugging. "So are you coming back tomorrow?" Her compliment opened the door for him to ask when he would see her again, which is a mighty flirtatious question.

Once you think of something you're truly grateful for and decide to thank someone for it, do it with enthusiasm regardless of how you think the person will respond. I've never heard anybody say, "I can't stand that woman because she's just so . . . grateful!"

Everyone likes to be appreciated, so don't be shy about it. The worst thing that could happen is that you'll thank somebody who doesn't know how to take a compliment, but that's their problem, not yours.

## Have a Flirting Contest

Flirting takes practice, and one unreturned smile or compliment is enough to send anyone directly to bed to hide under the covers.

But don't give up.

If you're tempted to retreat to the sidelines, one way to get back on the field is to get your friends to help you. To make flirting fun—and to laugh at the ups and downs—challenge your friends to a contest: Who can collect the most offers for dates over the next month? Get your creative juices flowing by turning on your charm. You don't have to *accept* all the dates—but you could if you wanted to.

The more conscious you are of being friendly and grateful and of making yourself as attractive as you can, the more likely that handsome guy will stop dead in his tracks when he sees you.

# 5

# ASK MEN TO ASK YOU OUT

*Believe me! The secret of reaping the greatest fruitfulness and the greatest enjoyment from life is to live dangerously!*
— FRIEDRICH NIETZSCHE

***Waiting for a man to ask you out can be a superhuman test of patience, but it's risky—and controlling—to do the asking.***

***The solution is to encourage men (or a particular man) to ask you out by asking him to ask you out. Send the signal that you're willing and available, then let him initiate the date. This will help you avoid an unnecessary risk of rejection, while encouraging him to pursue you.***

***Being pursued will make you feel desired, confident, and more beautiful.***

## Let Him Know You'll Say Yes

If you find a coworker attractive or wish the neighbor would stay a little longer, you may be tempted to ask him out on a date. Don't do it. Instead, smile and flirt with men you're attracted to, then ask them to ask you out on a date.

How do you do that? Let's take the man you see at your bus stop every day, for example. Let's say you bump into him five days a week and he flirts with you but never makes the first move. You can't make someone pursue you, but instead of sitting around like a potted plant waiting for him to take action, you could say, "I wish guys like you would ask me out," or "Here's my phone number in case you're interested in getting together."

These valuable phrases may seem outrageously forward, but they're subtle compared to asking him out for dinner. You're simply letting him know that if he offers to take you out, you'll say yes. That spares both of you rejection: He has a green light and need not worry that you will reject him, and you're not putting yourself in the direct path of "no, thanks." The ball is clearly in his court, but he's under no obligation to hit it back to you.

## Opposites Really Do Attract

> *Let us permit nature to have her way.*
> *She understands her business better than we do.*
> —Michel de Montaigne

Since you can't control who's going to be attracted to you, the surrendered approach is to accept or reject the invitations you get, rather than trying to force ones that aren't forthcoming. Instead of wasting time thinking about guys who you wish would ask you out but who haven't, control the only thing you can: yourself.

You might argue that asking men out is also within your power, but I don't recommend it. While the aggressive approach might be highly effective in the work environment, where survival of the fittest rules and masculine qualities are rewarded, dating is all about your powers of attraction as a *woman*. Since men are attracted to women in body, mind, and spirit, we appeal to them most when we're soft, gentle, and receptive. When you initiate a date, you take the role of the suitor and forsake the very thing that is most attractive to him—your feminine side.

However, inviting him to ask you out allows you to stay in the feminine position of receiving his offer while letting him pursue you. Starting off on that note gives the relationship the greatest chance of future success because it intensifies the powers of attraction. Opposites really do attract, but that doesn't mean you have to pretend to be anything you're not. Rather, honoring that you are a woman simply means that you admit that you like to feel admired and desired. That's exactly how you feel when a man asks you out.

If you do the asking, you'll miss out on the high of knowing you're attractive and desirable.

Since you're setting a tone for the entire relationship with this first date, using a feminine style and letting him have the masculine part ensures the greatest mutual attraction now and in the future.

*But*, you might be thinking, *I thought men liked to be asked out on dates.*

They do. Who wouldn't? It's flattering to know that someone admires you. However, men are less likely to be romantically interested in women who ask them out. They might not admit that they feel emasculated when they're in the receiving position or that they feel less attracted to a woman who does the pursuing, because she appears less feminine. They'll say something else, perhaps cite some tragic flaw, claim he lost her phone number, or admit that he did see her for a while—but only for sex.

Rather, men commit to women who *make themselves available* to them.

The difference is subtle, and men don't always notice it, but it is important.

I was talking about this phenomenon once when my brother's friend, Jeremy, told me that his fiancée *had* asked him out first. I asked him to describe his first meeting with her. Here's what he said: "She came up and introduced herself to me. She said she'd heard good things about me and wanted to say hello. So we talked for a while, and then she gave me her phone number, so I suggested we go out to get dinner, because I knew she wanted to go out with me."

I had to laugh. His perception was that she asked him out, but in fact, the key to their happy story is that *he* suggested they go to dinner. His future fiancée did make herself available, but when it came down to it, Jeremy was the one who actually initiated a date.

## Throw Out Your Running Shoes

> *Life demands from you only the strength you possess. One feat is possible—not to have run away.*
>
> —Dag Hammarskjöld

Making yourself available to a man means lingering to talk at a party or saying it would be nice to see him again. It includes receiving his compliment or his help graciously and looking your best when you know you're going to see him. Being available even translates into giving him your phone number or telling him that you wish someone like him would ask you out. It might involve telling a third party to ask him to ask you out (just like in junior high school).

If you run out the door before he has a chance to ask you out, you didn't make yourself available. For instance, Anna noticed that as she smiled at an attractive man at the gas station, he smiled right back. But then she got nervous and uncomfortable and started walking faster so she could get in her car and get away.

Muriel was at a crowded pizza place when a man who was also alone offered to share his table with her so she could sit down. Muriel, dreading the awkwardness that she anticipated sitting with a stranger, quickly said, "no, thanks" and took her food to go. Naturally, neither of these women got dates, and both regretted their knee-jerk actions.

Even if you're nervous, the trick is to drop the control, throw away your running shoes, and linger. Keep smiling and let the conversation lull. If he's going to invite you out, you want to give him the time and space in which to do it.

## Do as I Say—Not as I Did

You have tremendous influence on whether a man will approach you, but you can't control whether or when anyone will ask you out. Surrendering means being patient and willing to accept that you may never go out with the guy you have your eye on. Although you're relinquishing the control you could have if you actually took the reins and did the inviting, you will retain tremendous power by waiting for a man to pursue you.

That's a huge gain for a small loss of control.

When I was dating, I didn't know anything about surrendering or making myself available. Since I couldn't stand to relinquish control and wait for an invitation, I invited men out on several occasions. When they did accept, the possibility for romance always ended with that one date. I remember being at a Chinese restaurant with a guy I'd asked out. Maybe he agreed because he was flattered, or maybe he didn't know how to say no. Whatever the reason, it wasn't because he was interested in me romantically, and that became evident as the dinner progressed. It was uncomfortable for both of us and disappointing for me.

By asking him out, I thought I was staying in control of my love life, but what I had really done was expose myself to unnecessary rejection and heartache. If he had approached me for a date, I would still have been somewhat vulnerable to rejection, but his interest in me would have been much higher.

When I first met John, I unconsciously made myself available by saying, "I would love to go to a play sometime" during a conversation about the local community theater. His next sentence was to ask me to go to a play with him that Friday night. He would later tell our friends that I had looked him in the eye and said, "I wish someone would take me to a play," which gives you an idea of how effective making yourself available is. In his mind, I lobbed him a softball and all he had to do was hit it back.

Sarah found herself attracted to a tall accountant at a party. So when she was leaving, she walked up, handed him a piece of paper, and said, "I enjoyed meeting you tonight, so here's my phone number if you're interested in getting together again." He called, asked her on a date, and now they're married.

Kelly had enjoyed her conversation with Steve so much when he came to fix her mother's phone that she asked her mother to give him her phone number the next time he came by. Steve responded to this encouragement by calling her and asking her to come out to dinner with him.

In each of these stories, the option of getting together was left with the man. Although he had tremendous encouragement from the woman in each situation, he had to make it happen. That's what makes being available different from pursuing a man.

## When the Phone Doesn't Ring, It's Not About You

*There is only one way to happiness, and that is to cease worrying about things which are beyond the power of our will.*

—Epictetus

If you do decide to hand out your phone number, keep in mind that it might be a while before he calls. In fact, for any number of reasons, he might never call, which is why it's best to keep smiling and flirting wherever you go rather than wait for the phone to ring. The man you gave your phone number to might be seeing someone or recovering from a bad breakup. He could be gay, leaving the country, or an international secret agent who can't risk having you discover his true identity.

And, okay, it could be that he just wasn't attracted to you. But why tell yourself *that* when it could be anything?

Keep a positive outlook. Don't brood about the one who got away. Move on to the next opportunity.

Regardless of the reason, when a man doesn't call you after you give him your phone number, you haven't lost anything. There never was a possibility of romance with him—he wasn't available. The good news is that you didn't risk too much by giving him your number. You didn't have to go on a miserable date like I did, where my self-esteem rushed to my feet and leaked out of my shoes long before the waiter brought the check.

So keep moving! Keep smiling at every guy and don't stare at the phone. Say what the woman at the DMV says when her window is free:

"Neeeeeext!"

## Say "Yes" on the Spot

Remember: You can smile and flirt all you want without feeling any obligation to anyone. Flirting is attention without intention.

However, once you go beyond a smile and ask for a date or a call, you've given him encouragement and signaled an intention. Turning him down at that point would put you in the same league as Lucy when she encourages Charlie Brown to kick the football and then pulls it away at the last second. In a word, it's cruel. Once you've crossed the line from flirting to offering encouragement, the only fair thing to do is accept his offer.

Don't hesitate. Respond to an invitation for a date by saying "okay" or "yes" on the spot, if possible. Since part of being feminine is being receptive, receiving his offer on the spot will only make you more attractive. Playing games when he's already made an earnest invitation is going to send him a mixed signal. Since he's not yet entirely invested and prefers to avoid rejection, he may drop the ball. Don't risk it.

If you really have to check your calendar or rearrange your schedule, make it clear that you're willing to go out with him and give him your number so he can call to make a plan.

If you find that your schedules aren't matching up after you've given him a couple of dates when you're available, back off and let him propose a solution. He may suggest a date in two weeks when you're both free, rearrange his schedule, or promise to call you and firm up a time that works for you both. If he doesn't, don't fret; keep flirting with everyone you see. You only need to agree to things that fit for you, not bend over backward to make sure he gets to spend time with you. There are plenty of men who will find a way to see you if they know you're willing.

In fact, now that you know how to invite men to invite you out, try to gather all the admirers you can, just for practice. After all, it won't hurt to be reminded how very attractive and desirable you are.

# 6

# RETHINK YOUR NEGATIVE BELIEFS ABOUT DATING

> *Cynicism is not realistic and tough. It's unrealistic and kind of cowardly, because it means you don't have to try.*
>
> —Peggy Noonan

*All the good ones are taken. Dating is uncomfortable. It's a waste of time. It's dangerous. It's exhausting.*

*If these thoughts are part of your mind-set, you need to rethink dating. Dating is about casting a wide net. It's about having faith that there is someone out there for you and knowing that you can help him find you.*

*Dating is not about him. That means it's not about amusing, entertaining, or impressing him. Dating is all about you—where you like to go, what you like to do, why you're attractive and desirable.*

*If you've been thinking dating is work, it's time to reframe: It's fun—if you allow it to be so.*

## Bad Dates Get More Airtime Than Good Dates

On the up side, dating may expose you to elation, rapture, and the story of the pompous man who came to my door, took one look at me, and didn't make eye contact for the rest of the disastrous evening. I was sure to get attention and a hearty laugh from my girlfriends. To hear me, you might think that I'd barely escaped the experience with my life. I'd make it very clear by rolling my eyes that I did *not* have a good time. I figured a dating horror story was more entertaining than the story of a good date, and telling it helped me form an instant bond with other women.

Bad dates always got the most airtime. So we'd knock ourselves out trying to top each other's stories, which meant we were talking ourselves into hating to date.

I may have been bored or disinterested on a date, realized that he wasn't attracted to me, or felt nervous about the impending good-night kiss, but that's about the worst of it. If I'm honest about some of the dates I put in the "bad" category, I have to admit that I enjoyed seeing Cleo Laine in concert and going to an expensive French restaurant. I never was subjected to anything truly awful, not even once.

The risk associated with dating makes some people say that relationships are hard. "Yes, hard, so hard, like sleeping-on-the-floor-the-rest-of-your-life hard," one woman lamented. What she was really saying is that dating is uncomfortable because you can't control the outcome. You could be rejected.

True. For instance, when an attractive friend of a friend asked Samantha out, she got her hopes up. Luke took her out on Saturday night, was a perfect gentleman, and they hit it off. Naturally, she was excited about him.

Then she never heard from him again.

Samantha felt disappointed and doubtful about herself. She thought she was unattractive, too talkative, too homely, too boring, too nerdy. She had to admit to her friends that he never called, which made her sadness even more acute. She tried to brush it off as though it didn't matter, but she could not deny the feeling in the pit of her stomach, the pain of rejection.

Later she heard from their mutual friend that Luke got back together with his old girlfriend, but that didn't make her feel any less demoralized. She found herself wishing she had never put herself on the line, that he had never seen her as the eager puppy she admits she was that night.

## Cynicism Is Cowardly and Controlling

> *Worry is the price you pay for a debt you may never owe.*
>
> —Unknown

On the up side, dating may expose you to elation, rapture, and amazement. That's because it is often the first essential step toward falling in love.

Since dates are both essential for finding love and risky because of rejection, it's tempting to try to control the outcome of a date to protect yourself from disappointment. However, the only way for a date to be the start of something blissful is if you stay open.

Fortunately, in Samantha's case, in just a few weeks she had recovered from her disappointment and was seeing a man she met through work. "I realize I can't just stop dating," she told me. "It's the only way to get to know someone well enough to find out if you want to marry him."

Everyone faces the occasional disappointment when they're dating, but no one ever died of disappointment. Sure, it stings, and you might find yourself moping for a day or two (don't let it go on longer than that). After that, though, you can decide to move on with your life, and guess what? The sting goes away. Instead of thinking, *I might be wasting my time,* or *I might be rejected,* concentrate on how dating will lead you to the relationship you always dreamed of.

At the very least, each date is a life experience. You learn how to eat sushi or climb a rock. Maybe you're exposed to a live hockey game for the first time or see a silly movie you normally wouldn't have bothered with.

Most of all, dating provides you with *information.* You acquire invaluable insights about yourself that you can't get any other way, such as how you like to be treated and what qualities you're most attracted to—and what are your deal breakers. Surrendered dating teaches you things you can't learn any other way.

## Seven Fun Things About Dating

If you dread dating and expect to have a horrible time when you go on a date, you have a very good chance of being a prophet. Instead of setting yourself up like that, start focusing on the positive aspects of dating. Believing that dating is fun improves your chances of enjoying yourself on the date. This is important, because only fun dates lead to lasting romance. Can you imagine going out and having a miserable time with someone as a starting point for a long and happy courtship?

Fortunately, besides being risky, dating is also a lot of fun because:

1. It's flattering. Being asked on a date means you are attractive and desirable.
2. It's an opportunity to look your best, knowing that someone will be admiring you.
3. It awakens your hope and gives you permission to fantasize. How low can you feel on a day when you have hope that something good—or even great—is about to happen?
4. You're nervous and excited, like a kid on Christmas Eve, which is a wonderful feeling.
5. You're out in the world when you're out on a date, not passively sitting at home, wondering when you will meet your prince.
6. You get to try new things. Someone else buys your food and pays for your entertainment.
7. Dating is all about you: what you like to do, where you like to go, what you want to eat, who you want to be with.

## Negative Beliefs Are Not Realistic

*Many an optimist has become rich by buying out a pessimist.*

—Robert G. Allen

Maybe you have some negative beliefs about dating because in your experience, men just want to skip the romance and have sex. Perhaps your mother passed on to you the belief that most men are afraid to commit. Maybe you hang with a group of single women who are scared to get out there and so reinforce one another's fears by saying things like, "All the good men are already taken."

Maybe you've heard people say things like, "Realistically, I'm not going to meet and fall in love with someone after a certain age."

I always cringe when I hear that word *realistically.*

What they really mean is "I'm *afraid* that . . ." A more accurate way of expressing this sentiment would be "I'm afraid to risk my heart by going on a date, so I'll tell myself that I'm too old." Expressing fear as if it were a cold fact is pessimistic, not realistic. Pessimism fails to take into account human spirit and divine intervention.

The benefit of harboring negative beliefs is that once again, you don't have to risk anything. If you state your fear as though it's fact, you can wallow in the notion that there's nothing you can do about your loneliness but accept it as reality.

What protection! What a reason not to venture into the dating world.

Negative beliefs may feel like protection, but this kind of protection no longer serves you. To let go of a negative belief, simply replace it with a positive one.

Katie was afraid that a date who was taking her to a party with mutual friends might abandon her in the middle to go talk to other people. "Should I go off and socialize, too, so he won't think I'm too clingy?" She spent from Tuesday until Thursday *worrying.* She was trying to predict the future.

When she realized that she had a negative expectation about the date, she decided to tell herself something positive: "Everything will just flow naturally tonight, and I'll have a really great time." As it turns out, her date never left her side except to get drinks, and the two of them socialized with others together throughout the night.

Examine your negative beliefs about dating to see if you have been pessimistic or worrying. Here are some of the common unrealistic complaints that I hear from single women:

*Myth #1:* "All the good men either are taken already, don't want to get married, or are afraid to commit."
*Fact:* A friend of mine is a wedding photographer who works almost every weekend shooting happy couples of all ages on their big day. That's just the big weddings, too, and just the ones my friend photographs. If there weren't plenty of good available men who were willing to marry, my friend would be out of business. But he's not. He's only getting busier.

Go down to your local courthouse to see how many nuptials they perform. You'll find between dozens and hundreds of couples in a month, depending on the size of your town. It stands to reason that if people are getting married week after week, there still must be some good guys out there. As sure as there are people getting married while you read this book, there will be a new crop next month, next year, and ten years from now. Right now, however, they are single, eligible men.

*Myth #2:* "I'm too old to meet someone and fall in love."
*Fact:* If you read the wedding announcements in the local newspaper, you might get the impression that only young couples get married and anyone over thirty should just forget the whole thing. That, however, is not the reality. The new generation of brides' magazines—such as *Bride Again,* which is specifically for encore brides—demonstrates that advertisers are anxious to market to more mature women making wedding plans. That means there are plenty of them out there, and you could be next.

A ninety-one-year-old woman named Abby called to enroll in my workshop because she was concerned that her boyfriend, who was ninety-four, wasn't proposing. She explained that each of her three previous husbands (whom she had outlived) had proposed by this point in the relationship. She couldn't understand what he was waiting for. Needless to say, she didn't think she was too old to fall in love a fourth time, so why should you?

Abby is not the only person to fall in love after fifty. Elizabeth Taylor and Zsa Zsa Gabor both did it several times. Consider Gloria Steinem, married for the *first* time at age sixty. The *Los Angeles Times* recently ran a feature about people who find love at retirement homes.

It may even be that the older we get, the easier it is to fall in love because we grow more confident—and thus more alluring—with age.

> ***Myth #3:*** "I'm not pretty enough to attract the kind of man I want."
>
> ***Fact:*** First of all, you probably underestimate the degree to which a man would find you attractive. Women tend to be hard on themselves about their appearance. Men are fundamentally attracted to the female spirit as well as the female form. In her wonderful poem "Phenomenal Woman," Maya Angelou talks about how, although she was never good-looking, she always attracted the attention of the men in the room. If you've ever seen her, you know that her energy, confidence, and smile are uniquely feminine. She has a magnetic openness that draws in anyone in her presence.
>
> You have the same allure. Use it.

We've all seen a woman who is drop-dead gorgeous but can't seem to attract a man. Model curves and manicures won't invite a man unless her attitude is friendly and engaging. No matter how beautiful a woman, if she's scowling or standoffish, her chances of attracting a man are slim.

*Myth #4:* "Men just want to have sex."
*Fact:* Men definitely do want to have sex, but that doesn't mean they aren't interested in romance, too. If a man knows that you won't consent to having sex unless you're in a committed relationship, this becomes a nonissue. Men who really *just* want sex will move along, while men of substance will rise to the challenge of winning your trust and affection first.

*Myth #5:* "I might have to settle for someone boring."
*Fact:* What women are really saying when they express this fear is that they are only attracted to men who seem very exciting at first but turn out to be creeps. If you've been attracted only to creeps in the past, consider this: It's not the character defects you were attracted to before. Rather, you were probably attracted to his good qualities and later learned that he had some intolerable faults.

Let's say that you were drawn to his sense of adventure, like going for wild rides on his motorcycle. Then you realized he was hitting on every girl in sight when you were out together. It was the adventurous spirit you were attracted to, not his cheating heart. Maybe you liked the way a guy sweet-talked you but weren't so crazy about the way he stood you up after that. You liked being complimented, but not being all dressed up with no place to go.

In other words, just because some of the qualities you were attracted to happened to be attached to men who were incorrigible doesn't mean you can't have an exciting life with someone who's reliable and loyal. The two are not mutually exclusive.

I remember being nervous when John told me that I was so beautiful I was dazzling. *Uh-oh,* I thought. *Smooth talker!* I wondered if he was all talk, or a womanizer. But it turned out he was never so much as late picking me up for a date, nor did he hit on other women when we went out.

So if it's excitement you're looking for, you can find it in a good guy. Instead of being bored, you'll find yourself feeling that much more attraction. He will have the qualities you love and isn't going to let you down.

> ***Myth #6:*** "Men are intimidated by successful women."
> ***Fact:*** Men adore smart, accomplished women, so there's no reason to worry that you're too clever or successful to attract a man.

Tracy, a pretty forty-something, made a better-than-average salary at her glamorous PR job and owned a gorgeous home in high-priced Beverly Hills. When men didn't pursue a second date with her, she concluded they were intimidated by her success. "Men don't want to be with a woman who has a better car than they do," she told me.

It wasn't Tracy's success that scared men off. It was her aura of invincibility. From the way she acted, no one would suspect that she ever felt lonely, frustrated, wistful, awkward, or small. Instead, she seemed like someone who never felt anything less than competent, capable, and in charge. She was a woman who never allowed herself to feel vulnerable. Now *that's* intimidating.

Instead of assuming a controlling demeanor on dates, she would have been better off to reveal her softness and femininity. I am *not,* however, recommending that you dumb down or minimize your success one iota. Just remember that dates are neither job interviews nor networking lunches. What attracts others to us emotionally is our humanity and vulnerability, not our professional credentials. Therefore, while you're with a date, keep in mind that you do sometimes need a shoulder to cry on, a hearty laugh to join yours, and someone to share a sunset with. It won't make you weak, but it will make you softer.

> *Myth #7:* "Men like women who seem weak."
>
> *Fact:* Vulnerability—not weakness—is attractive, and you wouldn't want to manufacture vulnerability to elicit a certain response, because that would be manipulative. For instance, when Scarlett O'Hara told Ashley Wilkes how tragically lonely she would be without him, her sentiment was vulnerable, but her intention was clearly to coerce him into showing affection for her. As in all cases of manipulation, her motive was transparent.

Vulnerability, on the other hand, is authentic. When you let down your guard, intimacy and closeness spring from the relief of admitting you're not at all perfect and finding out that you're still lovable. Intimacy thrives when you relax in your own skin because you know you're safe.

I used to try to avoid vulnerability because I also thought it meant I was weak. Today I recognize that others find it endearing—not repulsive—when I'm honest and admit that I left the house with an extra pair of pantyhose stuck in the leg of my pants, or that I cried for twenty minutes after seeing a sentimental TV commercial. Even if it makes me burn with embarrassment, I consider my ability to reveal those tender feelings an asset.

Sometimes we try to avoid vulnerability without realizing it. For instance, one woman thought she was inviting intimacy when she said to her boyfriend, "I want us to be closer." She hoped that this would inspire him to say loving things and have long conversations, but it didn't. She was disappointed when he did little more than shrug in response.

What she meant to say but felt too vulnerable to reveal was that she missed him because they hadn't spent as much time together as she wanted. The tender message "I miss you" is much scarier to say because it reveals loneliness, which we tend to consider unattractive. But everyone likes to be missed, including the boyfriend, who, when she finally did say those three simple words, felt complimented. He responded by matching her sentiment. "I miss you too," he told her. "Let's go away for the weekened so we can relax together."

Being the first to be vulnerable in a relationship is not weak or manipulative. It is a great way to invite meaningful exchanges and heartfelt displays of affection.

Whatever your negative beliefs about dating, the good news is you can relinquish them and still be realistic. When you do, you'll be meeting and forming a relationship with a man you absolutely love in no time.

# 7

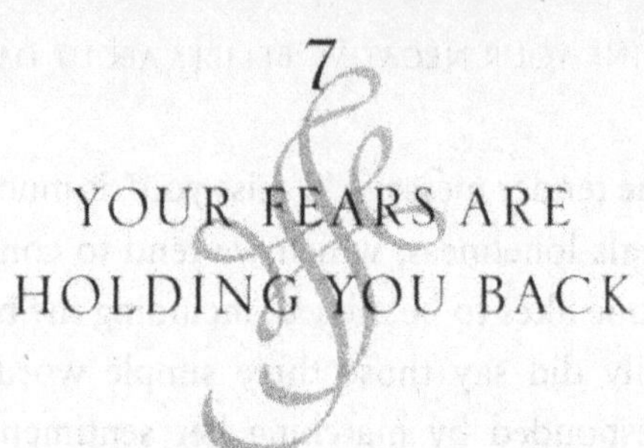

# YOUR FEARS ARE HOLDING YOU BACK

> *A lot of people approach risk as if it's the enemy when it's really fortune's accomplice.*
>
> —STING

***Feeling apprehensive or anxious are signs that you feel afraid. If you're thinking you never meet anybody or that your boyfriend won't commit, you may have more hesitancy than you realize about risking your heart.***

***No matter what stage your relationship (or lack thereof), your fears will keep you from progressing to the next level.***

## Becoming the Right Woman Means Finding Your Courage

You probably don't think of yourself as someone who's afraid to date or commit to marriage. If you can't seem to meet the right guy, however, it's probably not because there aren't any great guys available to date and marry.

"What are you talking about?" you might be saying. "It's really hard to find the right guy!" That may be. But another possibility is that your subconscious fears are keeping you from moving forward. This is especially true if you find yourself:

- rarely being approached for dates;
- turning down opportunities to date;
- going on lots of dates but hardly ever finding someone you want to continue dating;
- staying in or returning to a relationship that's unfulfilling;
- telling yourself you'll never get married;
- finding a new boyfriend every year or six months;
- waffling about whether you should marry your longtime beau;
- dating or living with a man indefinitely without getting married.

Even if it's just looking away when a stranger tries to make eye contact with you, your unspoken message to him is "Go away." These defense mechanisms are so ingrained you may not even realize they're there. But they're standing between you and the lasting love you say you crave.

If you're dating and not finding anyone worth committing to, your fearful belief is probably something like this: "You would eventually leave me anyway," or "I'll only get my heart broken."

You may tell yourself that no guy you've dated has been right for you, but if no mortal man can meet your standards, they're simply too high for a mere mortal man. You're using them to protect yourself from being disappointed. Perhaps that has kept the kind of man who's right for you from approaching you. Or maybe you've been out with someone who was terrific that you dismissed. You did this because you're afraid—not because absolutely everyone you've met has been substandard.

If you do form intimate relationships but don't stick with them, you may be using a defensive strategy that says, "I'm leaving you before you leave me," or else you pick men who are losers to begin with so that you can feel like you have the upper hand.

You can tell the difference by reflecting on your earliest feelings about him. Was it admiration for how smart and competent he was that attracted you? Or was it pity because he needed your help in some way? If you were drawn to him because you felt needed, you picked a man you feel superior to. You might feel safer with a man who seems to need mothering, but you'll never feel satisfied as his lover.

Dating the same guy steadily without ever working your way up to marriage is either about knowing that he's not the right man for you and hanging around anyway or fearing that your relationship won't stand the test of time. It could also be the fear of being alone that keeps you together. You're keeping one foot out the door so you won't suffer disappointment later.

You might use the excuse that men are the ones who never want to commit. Some men are confirmed bachelors and will never walk down the aisle. Hoping to get a commitment from such a man is a setup for failure and a waste of your time. There are plenty of guys who *are* the marrying type—when they find the right woman.

Part of being "the right woman" is overcoming your own fear of investing in a romantic relationship so that you can attract the right man.

## FEARS ARE NOT FACTS

*Optimism is an intellectual choice.*

—DIANA SCHEIDER

Before you can find the courage to overcome your fears, you have to know what they are. Until you consciously identify each and every one of your doubts, they will be difficult to override. That's why it's important to make a thorough inventory of what you're anxious about.

Here are some of the fears that women identify when I ask them to complete the sentence "I'm afraid that if I meet and marry a man I love . . .":

- I'll have to live somewhere I hate;
- I'll have to support him financially;
- he'll be unfaithful to me;
- I'll have to do everything;
- I'll have to give up my life;
- he'll die;
- we'll get divorced and traumatize our kids;
- I'll get too dependent;
- he'll expect me to clean up after him;
- I'll find out I made a mistake/picked the wrong man/could have done better;
- he'll reject me;
- I'll be smothered;
- I'll lose myself;

- the sex will get old;
- I'll find out I'm the type of person who can't be married.

If you identify with some or all of these fears, you're not alone. No wonder you resist getting into a relationship. Why would you? According to these beliefs, you'd only be taking the first step toward ruining your life or giving up something dear to you.

Subconscious fears influence the way you behave every day. For instance, if you believe you'll have to clean up after him, because that's what happened in your first marriage, you're not going to be very enthusiastic about smiling at men to make yourself available. Why would you? So you can date, marry, and clean his toilets?

Or if you're convinced that your boyfriend is eventually going to reject you, then you'll resist making a long-term commitment to him because you're not a masochist and don't want to go through the pain of a breakup.

Fortunately, your fears don't have to be your reality. Facing them means you don't let them run amok.

## Uncover Thinly Veiled Phobias

When we're afraid of something, we generally come up with a rationale to justify the behavior rather than just admit that we're afraid. I had a thinly veiled phobia of marriage when I was single.

Most women want to get married, but I didn't. I craved a man's attention and devotion, but I was afraid of divorce. By the time I met John, I had already decided marriage wasn't for me. I was too afraid that I would end up like my parents, whose brutal divorce devastated the entire family. Above all, I wanted to avoid the years of bickering that finally deteriorated into mutual destruction, anger, and ugly resentment. My subconscious note-to-self read: Can't get divorced if you don't get married. I was also afraid that I would miss the glamorous, fun-filled life of a single girl. Why settle down at all? I thought dating one man after another without ever taking on the burden of a commitment was the way to really enjoy life as a modern woman.

To disguise my fear, I said that marriage was outmoded. I reasoned that since people live longer now than they did years ago, the challenge for a couple to stay together for life is too great. The more modern approach, I decided, was to be a *Cosmo* woman—one who knew how to drive a man wild in bed, enjoy casual sex, and wear a crocheted dress. I wasn't aware that my view of matrimony as old-fashioned was a thinly veiled divorce phobia.

When I started dating John, I told him about my resolve not to get married. He was elated that I had no designs on his future. I had just bestowed on him the freedom to be with me without pressure to make serious plans for our future. As far as I knew, I was sincere. He thought so, too, until he mentioned what I had said to his sister, Claire.

"If she's not interested in getting married," Claire asked him, "why did she bring up the topic of marriage?"

She had a point.

In the beginning, I was confused.

As soon as I knew I was rapturously in love with John, I completely reversed my position. More accurately, I acknowledged my true desires. I realized I wanted to be with him for the rest of my life and suddenly marriage didn't seem like such a bad idea. In fact, I very much wanted to have the permanence of a mutual commitment and to announce to the whole world that this man was special in my life.

Since I was only twenty-one when John and I met, I hadn't engaged in much casual sex or learned how to drive a man wild in bed.

Even the crocheted dress was not a realistic ambition for me. John's guitar playing and blue eyes and my hormones overcame the promise of happiness I associated with being an independent, modern woman. I was forced to reexamine my beliefs.

My fears about the risk and potential havoc of a marriage gone wrong were still alive and well, but instead of addressing them, I simply changed my rationale. Some people *could* stay married for life, I decided. Just because my parents, their siblings, and their friends weren't able to didn't mean that I wouldn't. I figured I could stay wedded to John because we were different. When it no longer served me, I took off the veil that covered my fears about marriage. My desire to experience the supreme intimacy of being husband and wife outweighed my fear of becoming an ex-wife.

While my confidence in the future success of my marriage was based on a foolhardy naïveté that I was somehow immune to the problems that plague nearly half of all couples in the U.S., it still launched me into the healing realm of intimacy.

As surely as cuts heal and bones mend with the right treatment, falling in love with John and having him love me back helped restore smashed parts of me to wholeness. Instead of continuing to suffer from and compensate for the wounds of my parents' divorce, I felt restored by the constant reassurance and rocklike steadiness of John's affection for me.

I also felt relief from my constant internal pressure to be completely independent. Hope for a lifetime of happiness replaced my formerly gloomy outlook.

To embark on an intimate relationship, you have to override your anxiety. Surrendering to the wonderful feeling you get from being loved and loving a man will help you find the courage to banish worry. As you continue to enjoy each other, your fear of divorce, having to clean up after him, or being rejected will diminish.

Focus on the euphoric sensation you feel when you're together and how much you'd like to have it in your life forever. You too can make the leap into the healing realm of intimacy.

## When Monsters Are in the Closet, Turn On the Light

*To believe yourself to be brave is to be brave; it is the only essential thing.*

—Mark Twain

Taking inventory of what you dread is the equivalent of turning on the lights for a child who fears a monster in the closet. When you pull your fears out into the light, they often lose their power. Sometimes you realize they don't even make sense. Just being aware of what your fears are may not give you the nerve to override them, but it's certainly a step in the right direction.

For now, work on identifying your fears. Next, change your negative beliefs into affirmations by writing down statements that are opposite of your fear. I'm not suggesting that your fears will leave you when you affirm the opposite. However, you can overcome them by making a conscious decision to do so. For instance, "I'll have to live somewhere I hate" becomes "I'll live somewhere I love."

Colleen was afraid that if she married Dan, she would have to move to Boston, which she hated. Knowing this, Dan suggested that they move to San Diego, but Colleen was afraid she would miss her parents and the seasons on the East Coast. "How do I come up with a positive affirmation about this?" she wondered. But Colleen also realized that Dan would happily live close to where she grew up and that her fear was of a worst-case scenario, not a likelihood. Whenever she felt herself feeling afraid about the location of their future home together, she reminded herself that she would most likely live somewhere that she loved. Most issues like this one are relatively easy to resolve, since the man who loves you will want to make you happy.

You might argue that affirming something positive in place of your fear doesn't really help, because the fear is still there.

Yet, while a belief might feel like an immutable fact, it's actually a choice. Just as the optimist chooses to believe that the glass is half-full, you can make the decision to believe, for instance, that you will enjoy a home you really like when you meet and commit to your beloved. Since you aren't even in that situation yet, it's not unrealistic to make the assumption that when you are there, it will be a good experience. You are simply choosing to focus your energies on the reality you prefer.

If I had been conscious of my fear that I would eventually get divorced because my parents did, I could have affirmed something like this: "I will find my own path to a long and happy marriage."

It turns out, that's exactly what I did.

# 8

# END FRIENDSHIPS WITH EX-BOYFRIENDS

> *A woman has got to love a bad man once or twice in her life to be thankful for a good one.*
>
> —Mae West

*An ex-boyfriend hanging around in any capacity is a liability to a single woman. He represents the past when you're trying to move into the future. Holding on to the faintest hope that love will rekindle with him consumes physical, emotional, and mental space. His presence prevents you from moving forward.*

*If you have an ex-boyfriend still lurking in your life, let him go to make more space for the man who's right for you.*

*You'll have an easier time moving on if you have several close girlfriends who support you. Form and maintain relationships with other women so you aren't tempted to fortify your support system with an ex-boyfriend. Make convening with your coffee klatch or your three best girlfriends a part of your weekly routine.*

## With Ex-Boyfriends Around, Who Needs Enemies?

Letting go is hard and lonely. But the gift of loneliness is that it motivates us to do something to soothe that pain.

When you break up with a man, you might be tempted to ease the loneliness by calling him—instead of doing something where you might meet other people. Rather than joining a book club with other women who could fix you up or taking yourself to the gym where men abound, you can simply pick up the phone and have the admiration you seek.

The trouble is, it's not really what you want.

Having an ex around leaves open the possibility that you could get back together with him, which insulates you from feeling the full sting of your loneliness. However, it's important to *feel* the loneliness instead of numbing it with a pseudo boyfriend. Loneliness is what propels us to go on a blind date or get up off the couch and go out to the Halloween party. It ups your motivation to flirt at the grocery store or put on makeup before going out to do the laundry.

One woman told me that when she went through a big breakup, she tried to be busy five nights a week. "The other two were torture, and I was always tempted to call him," she reported. "I started running to use up energy. Then, I met people, but those Saturday nights alone were killers." Because she was lonely, she kept flirting and stayed open to the possibilities until she met someone new. Making herself busy also gave her the opportunity to socialize, which gave her more opportunities to date.

## Take a Break from the Ex

Chara was particularly reluctant to end her contact with her ex-boyfriend Jonathan, because they shared a mutual interest in art films. However, as part of her efforts to make herself available to the right man, she agreed that she would at least tell Jonathan she wanted a break for a while. Six weeks later, however, Chara couldn't resist forwarding him an interesting article about an independent movie from Brazil. Of course, what she really wanted was to be in touch with a guy who she thought was perfect for her in every way except one: He wasn't willing to get married. "I want to keep in touch with Jonathan because he's a wonderful man," she argued.

However, saying a man is perfect in every way except that he doesn't want to marry you is like saying you like everything about the ocean except that it's wet.

Fortunately, Chara soon noticed that her relationship with Jonathan was unfulfilling because he was more than just unavailable—he was self-absorbed. When she tried to be friends with him, she realized he wanted to talk about himself all the time and wasn't a very good listener. She started to tire of his company. "I had built him up in my mind to be much more exciting than he really is," she admitted. "It was probably just the lure of a man who was unavailable."

Lynn was also reluctant to give up her friendship with an ex-boyfriend. She insisted that it wasn't holding her back and that she wasn't attracted to him anymore. She wanted to maintain their friendship because she knew he would continue to support her when she was struggling with her family and because he understood her history.

She soon realized, however, that she was turning down chances to go to dinner with her friends and meet new people because she was spending so much time with him. She also felt obligated to return his kindness when things went wrong in his life. Reluctantly, she decided to tell him she needed a break and that she would call him back when she was ready. Once she was in a romantic partnership with someone else, she reasoned, she could pick up the friendship right where they'd left off.

But when Lynn did start seeing someone new steadily, she realized she no longer wanted to continue a relationship with her ex-boyfriend. She discovered that she didn't need to feed her relationship with her ex, because her friends and boyfriend were enough to get her through even the worst fight with her mother. Having one man in her life was plenty, and that position was happily filled.

## Don't Return to the Scene of the Crime

> *Friendship often ends in love; but love in friendship—never.*
>
> —Charles Caleb Colton

You may be sorely tempted to contact a boyfriend who broke up with you to see if you can win him back, but I don't recommend it.

Shortly after Steve broke up with Stacy, her life took a turn for the worse. Her mother was diagnosed with cancer, and she needed support more than ever. In her needy state, she decided to call Steve for support. Steve comforted Stacy by taking her out to their old haunts. Seeing him and feeling so close to him when she was vulnerable made her want to rekindle the relationship. "I figured he still loved me or he wouldn't be spending so much time with me," she reasoned. When they ended up in bed together again, she figured it meant they were starting fresh, but Steve wasn't up for it. "I'm just not interested in being in a relationship right now," he later told her.

In truth, they didn't just "end up" in bed together. Stacy was using sex to try to persuade him to come back to her. The rest of her life felt so out of control that she wanted to pull him back into her life, by hook or by crook. But since she couldn't make Steve recommit to her, having sex with him only made her feel worse.

Granted, Stacy wasn't in the best state of mind to be meeting someone special, but Steve's rejection was a new reminder of an old, stinging wound. Now she had something new to recover from before she could turn her energy to attracting a man who would be right for her. Trying to hang on to someone who didn't want to be there was a terrible blow to her self-esteem. It does take time to heal broken hearts, so if you've got one to nurse, make sure your environment is free of ex-boyfriends.

If you really want to get back together with an old love with whom *you* broke up, go ahead and give it a try. You'll either remember why it didn't work before or find that you've both grown in ways that make you great together. If he's moved on, you won't have that chance anymore, but at least you can stop mulling over that option. You'll learn something either way.

Returning to a man who left you, on the other hand, is like returning to the scene of the crime and putting yourself at risk again.

## Get Comfort from a Woman

If your ex-boyfriend comforts you, counsels you, dries your tears, and alleviates your loneliness, consider leaning on a girlfriend or two for that support instead. The more girlfriends you have, the easier it will be to let go of an old boyfriend whom you're using for support.

Sure it feels comforting to be in the arms of a big strong man, but sharing intimate topics with a former flame—even if that topic is your relationship—is bonding with the wrong guy. When we do so, what we really want is not so much support as the spark to rekindle old flames.

Another woman can empathize by sharing her feelings and, best of all, provide emotional support that is clearly nonsexual. What's more, girlfriends will help set you straight when you've gone off the deep end. Here's why women are indispensable:

- When you're thinking of going out with the bad-news womanizer at work, they'll show you the light.
- If you've decided to stop seeing a promising prospect because he didn't meet all the requirements of your checklist, they'll help you keep perspective.
- If you should encounter disappointment on the road to attracting the man who's right for you, they'll help you grieve.
- When it's time to stop moping, they'll encourage you to come out.
- When you're feeling low, they'll remind you of your worth and their love for you without making you wonder if they're hitting on you.
- If you're around women with successful relationships, they can

give you invaluable guidance and maybe even set you up with good prospects.
- When you have good news on the romance front, they'll help you celebrate in a way no ex-boyfriend could.

## It Takes a Village to Raise My Spirits

*Fortify yourself with a flock of friends! . . . There is always at least one who will understand, inspire, and give you the lift you may need at the time.*

—George Matthew Adams

I know I can't possibly get all the support, laughter, conversation, listening, stimulation, compliments, and attention I need from just one person, but sometimes I forget that.

I have been known for trying to get the support from my husband that would be reasonable to ask of him *and* three girlfriends. John is a wonderful listener and understanding of whatever I'm going through, but my girlfriends offer a perspective that he can never give me: that of a woman. When I need to gripe about how hormones are making me cranky, get tips for finding the right shoes to go with a new outfit, or just chat for hours, only a girlfriend, sister, or mom will do. Sometimes I meet women who say they don't really have close girlfriends, and I wonder how they ever survive.

Perhaps you don't like to impose on your girlfriends when you're feeling down or confused, but real friendship grows when friends are vulnerable. That doesn't mean you have the right to complain endlessly or be self-absorbed, but it does mean letting down your guard long enough to show that you're hurt or discouraged. When you want a reminder about why in the world you would bother with dating, a good friend can help. Relying on several friends to support you through a crisis ensures that you won't wear out just one with your problems.

Remember that your friend will need your support in the future or has leaned on you in the past. That's the beauty of friendship—you carry each other.

You especially need the encouragement of other women in your life when you're embarking on a change.

Tapping into the wisdom of her women friends was key to Janice's success in attracting and maintaining a happy relationship with Barry. Three-times divorced at fifty-five, she knew she didn't want to repeat her past mistakes, so she turned to women for support. "If I want to discuss something, I ask somebody with a good relationship her opinion first, and I follow her advice," Janice reported. "It's working! I have this amazing relationship like nothing I've ever experienced before."

Janice had discovered the power of having marriage mentors—women who already had the kind of relationship she wanted—to advise and support her along the way.

Having girlfriends you can vent to and from whom you can seek reassurance is a critical part of having an intimate relationship with a man, because other women ground you in your feminine spirit. Talking about lipstick, the problem with balancing work and dating, pregnancy, strappy sandals, or other strictly feminine topics reminds you who you are. It's the boost you get from being at a baby shower with women of all ages, sharing the uniquely feminine experience. When you leave, you're likely to walk, talk, and think like the woman you are. The more feminine you are, the more attractive you'll be.

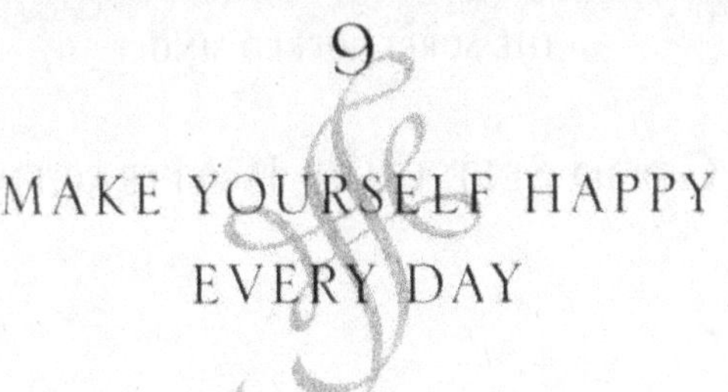

# 9

# MAKE YOURSELF HAPPY EVERY DAY

*It is not easy to find happiness in ourselves and it is not possible to find it elsewhere.*

—AGNES REPPLIER

*The more you enjoy your life, the more attractive you will be. Nobody wants to be with an unhappy pessimist. They don't make for good company. Make a list of twenty things that you can do to make yourself happy, then do three of them each and every day to boost yourself and your appeal to those around you, including those you have yet to meet.*

## Good Self-Care Is Attractive

In the movie *Broadcast News* Albert Brooks and Holly Hunter discuss how much easier life would be if only insecurity and desperation were attractive.

Truth is, they are as unappealing as rotten teeth. Like bad hygiene, insecurity and desperation reflect poor self-care. Both carry the sense that we are entitled to special treatment because we feel so bad. The only solution for either feeling is to take responsibility for our own happiness.

That doesn't mean you wouldn't ask someone else for help—only that you would let go of the illusion that it's that someone's responsibility to make you feel better. The best defense against the characteristic urgency of desperation is to proactively address your needs throughout the day, before you get to the very end of your rope.

So instead of saying to yourself, "If only that guy in accounting would ask me out right now, then I would be happy," say: "I've been working for three hours without a break. I think I'll take a walk to clear my head."

Self-care is anything that makes you feel good. For you, that might be taking a hot bubble bath, enjoying cookies right from the oven, taking a nap when you're tired. Or maybe it's the vitality you feel after you exercise, the cheer you feel from talking to an old friend, and the escapism of a movie or a novel. Self-care includes tuning in to your favorite TV show, going to the beach, relaxing by the pool, participating in sports, buying a new lipstick, taking a long lunch break, sleeping in, visiting an art museum, having your hair cut, buying new pillows, or even replacing your ratty doormat.

Practicing good self-care means you do at least three things that you enjoy every day. So if you're working full-time, going to school, and/or raising a child or two, and free time is hard to come by, you're going to have to *plan.* Decide ahead of time the three things for each day and then make it happen. If you're thinking there's no way you can find the time, consider Gina's situation.

Gina had a full-time job and was raising three children single-handedly. When she first learned about self-care, she insisted it wasn't possible to do even one thing for herself every day, except the one night a week when she stayed up late to watch her favorite TV show, but she promised she would try.

That week, Gina took longer showers so she could relax under the hot water for an extra ten minutes. She rented a book on tape that she'd seen at her neighborhood video store and listened to it on her way to and from work. She also made a point of lunching with a friend. Each of these activities provided a needed distraction. Life as a single mom was still hectic, but by the end of the week Gina appeared more rested and nourished.

The changes were small but powerful. She had given up her look of permanent exhaustion and seemed to smile more easily. Gina seemed alive, because she was enjoying life more. That made her more attractive, which wasn't lost on the men that she encountered.

## Self-Love May Feel Selfish

> *To love oneself is the beginning of a lifelong romance.*
>
> —Oscar Wilde

You may feel selfish when you practice good self-care. But keep in mind that you're not much good to anyone else if you're depleted, which is what happens when you don't practice some degree of "selfishness."

Karen felt guilty about taking time for herself, because she felt more useful if she did things for other people. "I like knowing that I'm needed," she told me. "But I tend to get cranky and resentful when I put everybody else before me, and that's not terribly virtuous."

Tired of hearing herself snap at other people, Karen decided that she would make herself do at least three self-care activities a day to avoid building up a resentment, just the way she would make herself floss her teeth. "I don't get as cranky, and I feel better about myself because of that," she admitted. "When I feel like I'm being selfish, I just remind myself that I'm on the right track for being a pleasant friend, coworker, mother, and possible love interest."

## TREAT YOURSELF AS WELL AS YOU WANT A MAN TO TREAT YOU

*I celebrate myself, and sing myself.*

—WALT WHITMAN

Without self-care, life gets drab. Once you've resigned yourself just to surviving the drudgery, you suffer a corresponding lack of vitality. Because you aren't enjoying anything, you feel listless and not interested in dating. You're either tired and numb or feel needy and anxious for somebody to come along and lift you out of your doldrums.

In contrast, taking good care of yourself reflects that you hold yourself in high esteem. That means that everyone around you—including the men you meet—will think of you the same way. Without ever saying a word, you'll be teaching the men who take you out to treat you as well as you treat yourself. If you're doing self-care regularly, they'll have to treat you very, very well.

Looking happy will help you attract the kind of relationship you seek, but there's another benefit too: Practicing good self-care is also a great way to establish an important habit you'll need for maintaining an intimate relationship with a man.

## Pursue Satisfying Work, Hobbies, and Friendships

Since vitality and passion for life are attractive, give some attention to your overall satisfaction with your work, your friends, and your hobbies. Are you doing work that you love, or do you suspect there's something better out there for you? Do you feel loved, supported, and happy after you talk to your friends on the phone, or do you wish they would find someone else to dump on? Are you involved in something enjoyable like a volleyball league, an art class, or a book club? Or do you find yourself going home to the TV night after night?

If you're a zombie every day after eight hours of work you hate, you won't be as vivacious—and therefore as attractive—as you could be. Good self-care in that case is putting together a new résumé and getting yourself into a happier situation.

If your friends drain your energy instead of filling you up, it's time to let your answering machine screen calls—and find some new friends.

If your apartment looks like you moved in last week and you've been there for three years, then good self-care would be putting in a few touches that reflect your style and say, "This is my home."

Preparing for an intimate relationship includes taking inventory of your life and letting go of things that don't fit.

But how does practicing self-care help with attracting a great guy? Since forming an intimate relationship naturally requires some energy, you'll need to make sure you don't spend all of yours working yourself silly. The better your life and the happier you are, the more likely you are to meet a man who fits right into that life and makes it that much better. If you're pretty miserable all around, you'll project that, too. Since people who are enjoying themselves are always more attractive than people who are just slogging through their day, you'll dramatically improve your chances of getting what you want romantically when you make sure that you're also getting what you want in the rest of your life.

# 10

# RECEIVE GRACIOUSLY

> *The feminine element in man is only something in the background, as is the masculine element in woman. If one lives out the opposite sex in oneself, one is living in one's own background, and one's real individuality suffers. A man should live as a man and a woman as a woman.*
>
> —CARL JUNG

*Make a point of graciously receiving everything you're offered, whether it's a stranger holding the door for you, a coworker carrying your laptop for you, or a friend who offers to pay for lunch.*

*Accept other people's thoughtfulness good-naturedly and recognize that receiving graciously is the ultimate act of giving up control. Receiving also honors your feminine nature by demonstrating that you can be soft and gentle.*

*Even if you're afraid you will be in debt to someone, receive his or her gift with open arms and gratitude. Respond to compliments by saying "thank you" and nothing more, even if you feel awkward.*

*Super-receive on a first date. It sets the tone for the rest of your relationship (if you decide to have one). Let him pick you up, open doors, pay the bill, do the work of keeping the conversation going, and kissing you if you want to be kissed.*

*Let him know, even subtly, that you expect to be treated like a woman. A good guy will have no trouble meeting your expectation.*

## Receive, Receive, Receive!

In Eastern philosophy, the concepts of feminine and masculine are called yin and yang. A comparative religion student once described these concepts to me this way: "Every object is comprised of yin (feminine) and yang (masculine). For a vase, the yang is the structure of the vase itself, and the yin is the empty part in the center. The yin is also the most important part of a vase because it is the part that can hold flowers. The yin is the part that receives, which gives the yang purpose."

The essence of feminine behavior is receiving. Traditional gender roles in dating also demonstrate this. The man escorts the woman, pays her way, and considers her comfort while the woman simply receives—if she knows how.

When you wholeheartedly allow a man to do these things, you feel special, protected, and cared for. It also gives him a sense of purpose and makes him feel more masculine even as it makes you feel more feminine. Thus, receiving is the perfect complement for the masculine spirit of the man you're dating.

When you resist receiving something, you reject the man who's offering it. For example, I saw a woman get on a crowded train with a bulky suitcase. As she found a seat and prepared to hoist her bag onto the overhead rack, the man in the seat next to her stood up and gently asked, "Do you want some help with that?" She denied herself the special treatment he was willing to give her by saying, "I've got it." With that she grabbed the handles and flung it onto the rack.

Granted, she was capable of lifting the bag herself, but by rejecting his kindness, she rejected her own femininity in a subtle but profound way. She also rejected his masculinity by leaving him awkwardly standing behind her watching her take charge of (yet struggle with) her luggage. He certainly wasn't suggesting that she was weak or incapable—she didn't appear to be either—rather, he was simply being the gentleman his mother or aunt taught him to be. Perhaps she was trying to be independent, but her response made her seem ungracious.

Rejecting the gift is rejecting the giver.

## If Receiving Is So Simple, Why Is It So Hard?

> *Life is under no obligation to give us what we expect.*
>
> —Margaret Mitchell

When I teach workshops, I ask everyone to participate in a receiving exercise by thinking of an authentic compliment for another woman in the class. Many women—married or single—can barely stand the discomfort they feel when receiving a compliment, so they make a joke or dismiss it, even though I've just reminded them to receive it seriously and thankfully. They always say the same thing: It is easy to give a compliment but hard to receive one. That's because we feel in control when we're giving a compliment and powerless when we receive one.

When you're smiling at every man you see and opening yourself up to the possibility of meeting the right man, more gifts come your way. Those gifts can include a smile from a stranger, a generous man giving you his cab when it's pouring. It includes compliments about your perfume, doors held open for you, and, yes, suitcases lifted to the overhead rack. These are everyday acts of kindness which, if you take them in, will remind you that as a woman you're held in special regard.

However, the other part of the equation is that people are more likely to offer "gifts" to someone whom they sense is open to them—someone willing to receive.

This is also true within a committed relationship. Whether you're just starting to date again, playing the field, or going steady with a guy, you'll want to brush up on your receiving skills to avoid inadvertently rejecting the presents—and the gift givers—that come your way.

Make "receive, receive, receive" your mantra.

## Excitement and Fear Are Two Sides of the Same Coin

Receiving means that you accept gifts courteously, whether it's something material (like a new sweater or earrings), an offer of help (like hauling a Christmas tree upstairs or changing a lightbulb that's hard to reach), or a simple compliment ("You've got a beautiful smile"). It sounds simple, but many of us are in the habit of dismissing and even rejecting gifts. Sometimes we're not even aware that we just rejected a gift.

Part of what makes receiving difficult is that we are not controlling what is offered, so any time something comes our way unexpectedly, we feel vulnerable—whether it's a free meal or a bouquet. If you accept the meal or the flowers, it means you have to acknowledge (at least momentarily) that you're deserving of those things even if you've done nothing to earn them. For those of us who were raised to always pull our own weight, that can be nerve-racking.

The thrill of getting a gift (and also the anxiety) is that you can't control or predict what it will be, so you have to accept someone else's vision of you, which can be tough. Even if their view of you is positive, if it doesn't match your view of yourself, you may feel embarrassed, exposed, or dishonest. Surrendering means relinquishing that control in favor of something better: the spontaneity and the emotional connection you gain when someone gives you a gift.

Accepting a seat on the bus is, in its own way, an intimate act. It's an unspoken acknowledgment of your femininity and a brief connection between you and the man who's offering his seat. It's not as significant as the intimacy of accepting diamond earrings from your boyfriend, but it is good practice.

When you refuse a compliment or a material gift, you are taking control of the situation. Now you've shifted the focus off from the giving and receiving (him and you together) and put it on you. In fact, the spotlight is now on your rejection, which will sting and overshadow the generous offer and the kindness behind it. Think of the man on the train who was just left standing there, watching the woman lift her bag.

## Good Receivers Have the Most Intimate Relationships

> *Love takes off masks that we fear we cannot live without and know we cannot live within.*
>
> —James Baldwin

Receiving can be a powerful way to connect with someone. Allowing a man to feel the pleasure of giving you something is potent. If you let him surprise you and find that you're authentically delighted, he will love knowing that he knows how to make you happy. You will feel wonderful knowing that he has studied you carefully and taken notes to become the expert on how to charm you. The more successful a man feels at pleasing you, the more likely he is to want to keep seeing you and keep pleasing you, and the more fun the two of you will have together.

So if receiving is so beneficial and seems so simple, why else, in addition to relinquishing control, do we have such a hard time with it? There are four reasons:

- We feel undeserving of what's offered to us;
- We think a gift will leave us owing a debt;
- We dismiss or reject a compliment in an effort to appear modest;
- We want to prove that we're independent and self-sufficient.

But none of these is a good reason to deny yourself a gift. Here's why:

### *1: You Deserve Sweet Things*

You deserve to have sweet, beautiful luxuries and affection in your life, and the people around you—particularly your boyfriend or the men you date—are entitled the pleasure of giving them to you.

You might not always feel that way, however. You may think it's too much trouble for him to come all the way to your house late on a weeknight so he can help you with a computer problem. You might think you don't really need an expensive trip to Hawaii when a weekend at the lake would be just as relaxing and he could save his money. Or you might feel guilty that he had to carry your pack and his on the last mile of the hike. However, the fact remains that you deserve to be treated to such gifts or he wouldn't be offering them. If you can't quite believe it yet, don't worry about it. Instead, act as if you believe it by graciously receiving as much as possible. Keep in mind that his gift giving makes him feel masculine, helpful, and strong. Your gracious receiving makes you more attractive to him.

Unfortunately, I had no concept of this when I was dating John. He would often tell me how beautiful I was. Internally, I scoffed at this idea, remembering the twenty pounds I wanted to lose and the three pimples on my chin. I mumbled something back, like "I don't know about that." In doing so, I denied him the pleasure of giving me the compliment; I denied myself the benefit of seeing my own beauty through his adoring eyes.

Now I'm much more in the *habit* of receiving graciously. That means that no matter how squirmy or uncomfortable I feel inside when a gift is offered, I make a decision to take it in as best I can. I don't want to miss the chance to connect with the giver—and have the gift.

I still feel nervous sometimes, but now I also enjoy the pleasure of the special treatment. When I decide to focus on the latter feeling, the former seems to dissipate anyway. I describe this concept to women in my workshops by telling them what I've experienced: that things will get as good as they can stand!

That was certainly Cheryl's experience. She was looking forward to moving into her fiancé's modest home after the wedding. But then he offered to buy her a bigger house—the one he knew she wanted. As soon as he mentioned the bigger house, Cheryl felt an urge to tell him that she could make do with the house he had. She worried that they couldn't afford it, for one thing. Because she'd spent most of her life in cramped apartments, she had trouble adjusting to the idea of such a large home. She didn't feel she deserved the big house.

When her fiancé reassured her that they could afford the house and insisted that he wanted to share it with her, she made a decision to receive. She thanked him, then tried to stay calm as he made an offer on the house she loved. As a result, she not only got the house but also the intimate connection with her husband-to-be, who was so happy he could please her.

### 2. *You Won't Owe a Debt*

Some of us live with this unspoken expectation that if someone gives us so much as a pair of socks, they expect something in return.

For example, Karen figured that the reason her boss gave her such a big Christmas bonus was because he expected her to continue to work late. In reality, her boss may have been hoping that she would continue to work late, but Karen's Christmas bonus had no such strings attached to it. By definition, gifts are free. The only strings attached to them are the ones we attach ourselves.

When a potential suitor or your boyfriend tries to give you something, you might be tempted to say, "Really, you shouldn't have gone to all that trouble," or "I can't accept that." Perhaps you fear that accepting a gift obligates you to do something for the giver, such as date, commit to, or have sex with him—but that simply isn't true. Nothing more is required of you when you accept a gift, unless a promise is attached to the gift, as with an engagement ring. The surest way to tell a man you just want to be friends is to offer to pay your half of the dinner tab on a date.

If a man offers to buy you a drink, receiving graciously means you accept the drink by saying "thank you." You wouldn't owe him anything, but you may decide to talk to him. You don't even have to drink the drink. If this same man asks you for your phone number, you can respond according to how you feel and what you want rather than from a sense of obligation.

As always, if accepting the drink would compromise your sense of safety in any way, then refuse it. If the man offering is drunk or seems creepy to the point that you don't even want to talk to him, *refuse his offer.* The rest of the time, however, you can accept with no worries. You don't owe him anything.

### *3. You Don't Need to Be Modest*

When it came to compliments, I wanted to let everyone know that I wasn't conceited. If someone said my outfit was pretty, I said it was old. If they complimented me for my accomplishments, I said that anybody could have done what I had done. If they said my home was lovely, I'd start on a litany of things I wanted to improve, just to be sure they knew I wasn't too full of myself. In reality, I wanted to move the attention away from me as soon as possible, because when the warm glow of the compliment spotlight was on me, I felt self-conscious and exposed.

If anyone has ever refused your compliment, you know how frustrating and disappointing it is. Likewise, your contradictory response to a compliment robs you of the opportunity to feel close to the giver. Now I realize that no amount of modesty is worth missing out on the connection I could have had. Today I reciprocate the gift by receiving the compliment gracefully, no matter how awkward I feel.

### *4. You Don't Have to Be 100 Percent Self-Sufficient*

If you're a modern working woman, then you probably take pride in your independence. You know how to take care of yourself and you're not afraid of being alone (although you prefer not to be).

That description fit Julie perfectly. She had a tendency to try to stay in control by never allowing a man to pay for her on a date. "I always feel that since I want to be equal I have to act equal. I also consider how much I have and feel that I can't take from someone who has less," she told me.

When she went out with Al, she made an effort to change her habit of keeping the score even and let him treat her. "He took the check and it was tough for me not to grab it. I sat on my hands and bit my tongue when the instinct to offer him money kicked in." And the whole time, she worried about the issue of equality.

A date is not a staff meeting. You don't have to earn your way every second when someone is offering you a gift. No one is judging you on your capability. Good guys don't offer things if they don't want to give them. A man who takes you to dinner is doing so because it gives him pleasure to be with you. Your presence, warmth, and graciousness are enough reciprocation.

I was so independent when I was single that I hated to admit that I ever needed help and hated even more to accept it. I thought taking things that others offered threatened my independence. I was determined to prove that I could do everything myself, and I viewed accepting help as a weakness.

When I moved in with John before we were married, I tried to split the bills down the middle, so that we each paid our share even though he was working full-time and I was in my last year of college. John offered to pay the bills in full so I could use my tiny earnings from my internship for spending money. I refused because I wanted to prove my independence. Looking back, I'm sure I could have used the respite from the constant financial strain, but I was afraid that accepting John's help would make me too dependent on him.

If I had decided to accept John's offer to pay the bills, I would have been dependent on him, but only for as long as I wanted to be. After all, I had clearly demonstrated my ability to support myself, and accepting his help wouldn't have made me less capable. Looking back, I think my inflexible approach had to do with wanting to keep some measure of control in the relationship. If I didn't rely on him, I could insist on having things my way. What I didn't realize then is that he only wanted me to be happy.

I hadn't learned anything yet about the fine art of receiving.

## Good Receivers Get More Dates

Tanya was just starting a new job when her coworker Mark called to ask her on a date. She accepted, but when another coworker asked, "Was that the Mark in the sportswear department or the one in scuba gear?" she realized she didn't know. "I guess I have a date with whichever one comes to get me on Saturday," she said, shrugging. It turned out to be Mark from scuba—and her future husband. Lucky for Tanya, she was happy to receive all the offers that came her way, even if she wasn't quite sure who they were from.

Ray tried to buy a glass of red wine for a woman who appeared to be single and alone at a restaurant (and who was already drinking red wine). The woman refused to accept the drink, which she had every right to do, and Ray did not pursue her further. We don't know this woman's motives for rejecting Ray's offer, but if you want more men to pursue you, then don't do what she did.

Even if you think you wouldn't be interested in Ray, accepting his wine and letting him approach you and even take you out is the very kind of experience that will lead you to the man who's right for you.

When you receive a man's gift, he's more likely to invite you on a date simply because you are receptive; you've accepted, not rejected him. Therefore, a good receiver will get more opportunities to date, which means she has a better chance of attracting the man who's right for her. If your goal is to be attractive to the right man, then make a habit of taking a feminine approach by receiving as much as you can. It's a way of saying to the world, "Let good things come my way!"

Some women worry that accepting gifts from a man you know you're not interested in is cruel because it gives him hope when he doesn't stand a chance with you. This is a valid concern. It isn't kind to string somebody along. However, it's not cruel to receive from a man when you're still making up your mind about him. If anything, rejecting his gifts while you're still deciding would be shortchanging yourself. Men woo women with traditional gifts, like dinner and flowers, and with more modern ones, like upgrading her computer or helping her with a work project. Receiving those things will make you feel special, but it won't put you in debt to anyone.

## You Can't Control and Receive at the Same Time

> *Often the prudent, far from making their destinies, succumb to them.*
>
> —Voltaire

You might be thinking you would never reject gifts from your man—if only he would give them. But some women who *feel* they never get gifts actually reject them on a regular basis because what they're offered isn't what they had in mind. In trying to control what they receive, some women discourage the gift giver altogether. The reasons vary from "I knew he couldn't afford it" to "I would never wear the shoes he picked out for me," or even "I refused to go to the movies with him because I'm sure he'd only want to see the latest action flick."

Perhaps you're thinking of situations where you feel you can't accept what your boyfriend is putting before you (i.e., he would spend everything and have no money for rent). Perhaps there are situations where you'll decide to reject his offers. The point is to recognize the cost.

For instance, if he struggles to make the rent but wants to take you out anyway, then you have a choice. You can either act like his mother and tell him he can't afford a night on the town, or you can be a good sport and enjoy the treat. If you try to force him to be more responsible by refusing to let him spend his money on you, you're not only passing up his gift, you're emasculating him by implying that you don't trust him to manage his own life.

When you receive graciously you are making a choice to open

yourself to intimacy. If you are already in a relationship, receiving signals that you are making intimacy the priority. So if you want to attract men and laugh with them instead of bickering, it's in your best interest to accept graciously whenever you can.

## Reasons to Reject a Gift

There *are* some gifts you will have to reject. For instance, you would have to reject a man who wants to give you a kiss when you don't want to be kissed. That engagement ring I mentioned before might be something you have to turn down if the man bearing it is not the one. The way to know when you should reject a gift is to ask yourself if it is coming with strings you're not comfortable with. In that case, just say no.

Otherwise, don't forget your mantra: "Receive, receive, receive."

## First Dates Are Critical Times to Receive

What makes a date different from every other social gathering between two people is that it holds the possibility for romance. Romance is composed of a masculine spirit meeting a feminine one in a way that's complimentary and exhilarating. To receive is to be feminine, while to demonstrate an ability to provide, please, and protect is masculine. A man may exhibit his masculinity in any number of ways, including:

- giving you his jacket because you're cold;
- bringing you flowers;

- pulling out your chair at dinner;
- paying for food and entertainment;
- walking you home;
- telling you how beautiful you are.

A woman who enthusiastically receives special treatment from a man on the first date is acknowledging that she likes to be treated thoughtfully. Since the first date sets the tone for the rest of the relationship, you're opening the door to romance—perhaps even a lifetime of it—by accepting these gestures. By contrast, rejecting chivalry robs you of the gifts your date wants to give you and simultaneously sends a message that you are not interested in a romance with him.

Patty discovered this when she insisted on paying her half of the dinner bill during her first date with Andrew. Suddenly, the playful, pleasant conversation stopped and Andrew was in a hurry to take her home. There was no good-night kiss, and he never called again. Patty said she was glad she discovered early on that he couldn't "handle" a strong woman.

She didn't realize that paying for her own dinner was a form of rejection.

Although her date had never said, "I'd like to treat you to dinner," that is what he meant when he asked her out. When she offered to pay the bill, the message she sent was "I'm not interested in special treatment from you." That meant there wasn't much room for him to try to please her by buying her dinner. After learning this, he suffered a corresponding drop in interest. In rejecting his gifts, Patty had rejected him.

As a modern woman, you are perfectly capable of paying your half of the check or finding your way to the movies. However, not only does every capable, independent woman need a little pampering from time to time, but every gentle, kind, understanding man needs the opportunity to stretch his masculinity muscles and demonstrate his chivalry. A first date is the perfect opportunity for everyone to step out of their capable, genderless work modes and embrace their respective femininity and masculinity. In fact, making a conscious effort to transition from your in-charge work self to your relaxed self before you go on any date will benefit you in several ways:

- The last thing you want to do after the work day has ended is keep running everything. Make it easy on yourself and let him treat you.
- Your date doesn't need you to manage him the way you manage your clients, children, or projects, but sometimes the habit is hard to break. Consciously switching hats will help you remember not to treat him like an employee or your son.
- Learning to transition from a woman in charge to a woman who likes to enjoy herself is a great habit to establish now, because it will help you maintain a happy marriage in the future.

Being in charge at work or at home with the kids may be a big part of who you are, but so is the part of you that likes to be taken care of. Learn to reveal the qualities that are most appropriate for the situation. You won't lose anything by letting him spoil you for the evening, but you will feel wonderful if you let him treat you like a woman.

As it turns out, the more you receive, the more he will treat you as though you're special, and the more feminine you will be. The more feminine you are, the more masculine he'll feel. Together, you'll complement each other beautifully.

# 11

# JUMP-START YOUR LOVE LIFE WITH A DATING SERVICE

*Adventure is worthwhile in itself.*
—AMELIA EARHART

***Feeling confident on a date and enjoying it takes practice. If you're in a dating slump, get things going in a hurry by joining a dating service or asking friends to set you up on blind dates. The sooner you start dating regularly, the more practice you'll get and the more confidence you will have on future dates.***

***Stop holding on to the idea that blind dates and dating services are for desperadoes.***

***They're not. They're practical.***

## START DATING NOW

To some women, joining a dating service seems desperate, unsafe, or tacky. But to the millions who sign up and upload their pictures to Web sites, a dating service is a great way to make yourself available to men in the modern world. Taboos are fading as women realize there are plenty of attractive, available men in online dating services.

Besides, everybody else is doing it (even if they're not talking about it).

If you feel self-conscious about joining a service, you don't have to tell anybody. Only your computer will know. You can even join a service specifically for Surrendered Singles at www.surrenderedsingle.com.

A dating service is an effective way to overcome your fears and introduce you into the flow of receiving and romance.

Here's why I strongly recommend joining one (at least):

- **To get dates fast:** Joining a dating service is an immediate source of contact with men who are also interested in dating. Now you're empowered because you're no longer sitting at home, waiting for the phone to ring. You're taking control of your life, which is the only life you can control.
- **To give you lots of options:** If you have only one dating prospect, he's the one you tend to focus on. A dating service gives you many options, which keeps you from getting stuck on one guy and eliminating other possibilities.
- **To boost your ego:** Instead of staying at home and secretly wondering if anyone would want to go out with you, going on dates reinforces that you're desirable.
- **To conquer self-sabotage:** If you're feeling shy, scared, or out of

practice about flirting, you may be sabotaging yourself and preventing dates from coming your way. Joining a dating service allows you to announce your availability to other available people.

- **To awaken your feminine energy:** If you join a dating service, you *will* get dates. And going on them will help you tap into and exude a more receptive, soft, gentle energy that lasts long after the date is over. For days afterward, you'll find men are attracted to you wherever you go, because you've become more feminine. The sooner you start dating, the sooner you start magnetizing men.
- **To provide an opportunity to practice:** You can change your dating habits by applying what you learn from this book—but only if you have dates to practice your skills on.

## Take Action to Make Yourself Available

*A ship in harbor is safe,*
*but that is not what ships are built for.*
—John A. Shedd

Taking a proactive approach toward dating doesn't mean you have to do the hunting. A feminine approach still requires action, but it's the action of making yourself available. This is one of the reasons I think dating services are great: You make yourself unequivocally available to lots of men in one fell swoop.

I favor online dating services over personal ads because they provide a huge pool of potential dates. They also may give you a greater measure of safety because you can read about your prospect before you respond to his e-mail.

In addition to joining a dating service, you could ask friends to set you up on blind dates as a way of getting out there and dating now. Anything that provides you with several men who are interested in dating you is a good bet.

## The Man Who's Right for You May Find You Without Logging On

*The absolute yearning of one human body for another particular body and its indifference to substitutes is one of life's major mysteries.*

—Iris Murdoch

Joining an online dating service was especially helpful for Kathy. She was doing her best to flirt with every man she saw by smiling at them all when she went on her daily walk around her neighborhood, but she complained that most people weren't smiling back. It wasn't until her sister came along on the walk that she discovered why. "You keep your head down until the very last second," her sister told her, "and then you say 'hi' with this deep, otherwordly voice that scared the stuffing out of me the first time I heard it."

Clearly, Kathy was feeling conflicted about the idea of letting people know that she was available, and it showed.

When she put her profile online, however, men came to her. All Kathy had to do to get past her reluctance was respond to invitations to go out. Her first date was with Jeff, a perfect gentleman who opened doors and took her to a fancy Asian restaurant. Although there were no fireworks that night, Kathy was happy to sit and talk with him after dinner and enjoyed herself so much she was surprised to learn how late it was. Another man who took her to dinner kept her laughing by telling her about embarrassing things he'd done at work. Neither date turned out to be the beginning of a romance, but each brought Kathy a night of lightness and fun with a man, which she hadn't had in a while. More important, it reminded her that she enjoyed holding her head up high, making eye contact, and being out.

These experiences left Kathy feeling emboldened. "Dating wasn't as hard or as scary as I had made it out to be in my mind," she admitted.

The dates also served to remind her of her feminine nature, from her desire to be adored to the sway of her hips. Ordinarily she assumed a businesslike persona that was effective at work and when trying to get the landlord to fix leaky faucets, but not at all useful for sparking romance. After going out on a few dates, she was conscious of her own powers of attraction. She found it easier and natural to smile and even flirt with men she encountered every day, because she felt appreciated by men in general. "I've noticed that when I'm out walking now and smiling at men that they're mostly smiling back," she said.

Joining a dating service will give you a chance to practice flirting and make you feel feminine just as it did for Kathy. Once you own that part of yourself, everyone else will recognize it, too. As a result, you'll begin to magnetize men to you wherever you go.

So even if the man who's right for you never joins a dating service, he'll be attracted to you when he sees you at the bookstore, in the laundry room, or on the beach.

## Make the Most of Your Dating Service by Doing the Least

Getting calls from a man through a dating service is less terrifying than making eye contact and smiling at a stranger, but not much.

When Jerry called Liz after seeing her posting, she was nervous, so she suggested they get together for coffee as a way of getting off the phone quickly and controlling the outcome of the conversation. They had a nice time, so when he asked her out for the following weekend, Liz accepted. He said he would look into what concerts were coming up and then added, "We have each other's phone numbers." She hoped that meant he would call her, but he never did.

"I made myself available to go out again, but he didn't respond," she complained. But Liz had done more than make herself available—she had gone out on a dangerously long limb and taken the unnecessary risk of *initially* asking him out when she suggested coffee. Of course, he was probably calling to ask her out, but he didn't get the chance because Liz controlled the situation. Granted, she didn't force him to go to coffee against his will, but she did start calling the shots before Jerry had a chance to invite her out. By stepping into the dominant role, she put him in a receptive roll, which is emasculating. No man enjoys feeling emasculated.

Jerry's comment about their having each other's phone number was certainly ambivalent. Perhaps initiating dates wasn't Jerry's strong suit, in which case maybe he never would have suggested they get together in the first place. Liz spared him the trouble, but she also denied herself the opportunity to see what he was made of. She didn't let him take the reins and as a result, she learned that he wasn't the kind to step up to the plate *after* she'd already invested some effort in him.

For whatever reason, there are guys who call women but don't ask them out. You don't have to waste your time with them, because there are plenty of men who will show their strength and do their part without any help from you.

## Ignore Invitations When You're Overwhelmed

A Surrendered Single resists the urge to pursue men online. Initiating dates or pursuing men on dating services is no different from asking a man you meet in the "real-world" for a date. It puts you at high risk of rejection and robs you of the opportunity to feel desired. Therefore, instead of reading the ads men have posted and contacting them, let the ones who are interested read your ad and come to you.

That's what Carol decided to do, and since she received over one hundred responses from her Internet dating service in three weeks, she had plenty to choose from. "I got overwhelmed and stopped responding to any of them because I couldn't keep up with them," she fretted. "I'm so used to taking care of men, I was worried I'd crush the ones I didn't respond to. Now I realize it's okay—they don't even know me, so how can they be upset if I don't respond to them? I had to acknowledge my limits and take care of myself by just answering three or four a week by sending my cell phone number so they could call me. I don't even leave my cell phone on most of the time, so I can screen the messages before I respond to them."

Your dating service is strictly for your benefit, not an obligation to perfect strangers. If you find yourself overwhelmed with potential suitors, practice good self-care by responding to only enough that you have the chance to go on some dates, enjoy the male attention, and be reminded of what a delightful, desirable woman you are. You can ignore all the offers beyond that.

## Ending the Call Without Ending the Romance

Liz decided she no longer wanted to risk rejection by initiating first dates, especially since men were calling and being direct about asking her out. Thanks to the responses from her dating service, she knew she had lots of options. This made her disappointment about Jerry sting less.

Now, however, Liz had a new problem. "How do I ever get off the phone?" Liz asked. "Some of these guys will talk for an hour, and I just don't want to talk to a stranger that long." Of course, there's nothing wrong with staying on the phone as long as you're enjoying yourself. But since Liz didn't enjoy long first phone conversations, she decided to let callers know up front that she only had fifteen minutes to talk. "I tell them, 'I can only talk for a few minutes,' and to myself I think, *because otherwise I start feeling irritated about being on the phone so long.*"

To ensure that she made herself available during these shorter phone calls, Liz would end the call by saying, "I have to get going. What do you want to do next?"

"If he said, 'Let's go to the movies on Saturday,' then great," Liz reasoned. "If he didn't offer any suggestions, I figured there was some kind of holdup on his end. So many men were contacting me from the dating service, I realized I didn't have to fret about the held-up guys. I'd just wrap up the call, shrug it off, and talk to the next guy."

Liz found this approach empowering. By responding to calls in a way that was feminine, available, and mindful of her own desires, Liz set herself up to meet a man who was right for her. She also didn't waste time and energy talking to men who might never step up to the plate and ask her out.

## Lower the Drawbridge

> *The most important things to do in the world are to get something to eat, something to drink, and somebody to love you.*
>
> —Brandan Behan

Tom was one inch shorter and two years younger than what Dina specified she wanted in her profile. That didn't stop him from contacting her through the Internet dating service they both belonged to, and it's a good thing. They hit it off and now they're engaged. Now Dina realizes that her age and height requirements weren't all that important. "I just put in numbers because they ask for that information when you're filling out the form," she said. "I'm so glad Tom paid no attention to that!"

I've seen profiles that specify not only age and height, but personality traits, hair color, and income. Talk about a checklist. When I see these postings I think, *This woman is ruling out a lot of perfectly good men.*

Unless you're inundated with responses like Carol was, stay open to the possibility that the man who is right for you might be very different than what you imagine. While you may be tempted to try to avoid falling in love with a man who's younger or who has less education than you by setting a certain standard, I don't recommend it.

Remember that the reason for using dating services is to make yourself available. Wiping out 99 percent of the population with impossible standards defeats that purpose. Since you can't control who is attracted to you, just receive all the attention you get and enjoy it by reminding yourself that you do have the power to reject anyone you don't find attractive. Even if you can't respond to everyone, you'll feel good knowing that with all the e-mails in your box the line of men waiting to talk to you would wrap around the block.

### Present Yourself Plainly and Playfully Online

When you write your profile for a dating service, focus on describing yourself instead of what you want him to be like. Be:

- *playful,* to show that you know that dating is fun;
- *brief,* to show that you understand there's no substitute for spending time getting to know someone;
- *inviting,* to reveal that you're open and feminine.

Here's an example of a playful profile that attracted hundreds of replies for one woman on Match.com:

> "I love being in a romantic relationship. That sums it up! Just kidding . . . there's more. I love having fun. I especially love it when there's chemistry with a guy I'm with. I love to explore the world and also the simple pleasures of life. I thrive with men

> who are gentlemen and enjoy the differences between the sexes. I'm good-hearted and can be considerate (I think?!!). I like people and enjoy socializing, but I also like private social times as a couple. What can I say? I'm a true Libra."

Another woman effectively revealed some vulnerability in her profile when she included this sentence: "I am new to this way of meeting people, so if I'm slow to reply or a tad shy, it's just because I'm not used to this."

What man wouldn't want to try to make her feel comfortable, knowing that she's not used to online dating?

Both listings included a flattering picture of the woman. Your picture will tell a prospective date more about you than just your looks, so be thoughtful about yours. I've seen some that show the woman holding a wine glass or beer bottle, or with a man's arm around her shoulder (he's mostly cut out of the picture, of course), which I don't recommend. Others run pictures of themselves looking very serious or sulky, or shying away from the camera. Some might call it arty, but appearing moody doesn't make a woman more attractive. One woman posed suggestively in a skimpy outfit, as if to say, "I'm a sex object," while another woman hunched behind a desk in a bulky tweed jacket to send the message "I never leave the office." Still others were so blurry and dark that they resembled the images from the FBI's "Ten Most Wanted" lists.

You don't need to be tap dancing, snorkeling, in soft-focus, or standing in front of a mansion to make yourself seem impressive. Ideally, your picture will be a simple, clear shot of you and you alone. You'll be smiling and looking into the camera on a day when you're looking and feeling good.

Your future husband will have an easier time finding you if you leave the drawbridge down so he won't have to swim across the moat.

## Jump-Start Your Love Life Right Now

So, have you joined a dating service yet? Asked friends to set you up on blind dates? There's no reason not to take action right now. So go ahead and do it—I'll wait.

The sooner you make yourself available, the sooner you'll attract the man who's right for you.

# 12

# ACCEPT DATES WITH MEN YOU NORMALLY WOULDN'T GO OUT WITH

> *We come to love not by finding a perfect person, but by learning to see an imperfect person perfectly.*
>
> —ANONYMOUS

*Give up your preconceived notions, conjectures, and snap judgments about men who ask you out. Accept all the offers that come to you unless he's the creature from the Black Lagoon. Remember that he's not asking you to spend the rest of your life with him—just a few hours. You have nothing to lose, but you will make progress toward meeting the man who's right for you by getting out there and practicing receiving graciously.*

## Going on a Date Is Not Going into Debt

Now that you're smiling at every man you see, telling people to fix you up, and participating in your dating service, you're going to get invited on more dates, which is great. You might be tempted to say "no, thanks" when you think there's no chance of a future with a particular guy. Instead, consider going out on all the dates you can. After you cast a wide net, take a look at the bounty. You may be pleasantly surprised by your catch.

One benefit of accepting all the dates you can is that you won't prematurely rule out a man who's right for you. You're giving everyone a chance, and in so doing, you're letting go of your prejudices, assumptions, and quick judgments about them. Whatever your prior experience with a certain man, you'll be able to make a more informed judgment about him after you've spent an evening together.

Another reason to accept dates is that you can use the opportunity to practice receiving graciously, since he'll be paying for dinner, opening doors, and bestowing compliments. Get used to saying "Thank you!" instead of "That's okay" or "I'll get it."

Going on a date with someone you might have refused before is simply about resigning your judgments—not your whole being. Remember that just because you agree to go out on a date with a guy doesn't mean you agree to anything more than spending some time with him. You haven't committed to kiss him, to go on a second date, or to do anything else. You certainly don't owe him anything. Paying for the date is his wager that he can win your affection, and you are being fair simply by giving him that opportunity. There are no strings attached to what he gives you, so don't attach any yourself or act as if there are.

## YOUR PERSONAL COMING-OUT PARTY

> *It had been my repeated experience that when you said to life calmly and firmly (but very firmly!), "I trust you; do what you must," life had an uncanny way of responding to your need.*
>
> —OLGA ILYIN

Most important, accepting dates liberally helps you get into a groove. You've probably had prior experience with this groove. It's when you suddenly go from having no promising prospects to having several men pursuing you at once. Being in the groove is the manifestation of that old expression "When it rains, it pours." When you are being wooed by a man, it awakens your feminine energy and confidence. Even if you're not interested in someone, it still feels good to know he's interested in you. That knowledge triggers you to "send out your scent," as my friend Candace would say. What she meant was that it lowered my defenses and replaced them with openness and a self-confident glow.

Knowing that a man is enamored of you reminds you that you're attractive and desirable. As a result, you walk taller and smile brighter. Your body language is open. You're sending out the message that you are receptive. That's why just knowing some man somewhere is interested in you will make you more attractive to all the other men you encounter. Thus, accepting a date from a man—any man—can help you attract other offers.

That means it's in your best interest to accept an invitation, even if it's not from a hot prospect. Look at it as practice or consider it the kickoff to the dating season. Think of it as your own personal coming-out party. It doesn't matter who you come out with, as long as you come out and let everyone know that you're available.

Cora wasn't particularly interested in any of three men who had asked her out, but she accepted the dates to give herself a chance to dip her toes in the dating pool again. She told herself the dates were a good opportunity to wear clothes and makeup that made her feel beautiful and to enjoy being admired. Cora was already feeling attractive and feminine when her date introduced her to his acquaintance, Brad, at an art gallery. The following week, she ran into Brad again while they were both scuba diving. He remembered her from the art gallery and struck up a conversation. They got married just over a year later.

Petra had a different reason for being glad she accepted all the dates that came her way. She had just met Stuart and was so excited about an upcoming date with him, she almost didn't waste her time with George, whom she thought was too quiet and not her type. Still, she realized her relationship with Stuart was far from certain, so she agreed she would let George take her out for dinner. She was surprised to find that she enjoyed their evening together and found herself laughing and appreciating his efforts to keep her entertained and comfortable.

Then came the big date with Stuart, who called that afternoon and asked her to meet him at the club because his schedule was tight. Not wanting to put the long-awaited evening in jeopardy, she agreed. But when she got there, Stuart was already deep in conversation with a group of friends. He spent most of his night chatting with them and showed little regard for Petra. After both dates, not surprisingly, she had a higher opinion of George than of Stuart. Now imagine if she had turned down George. That night with Stuart would have been disappointing, if not downright heartbreaking. Having George around softened the blow and kept Petra's spirits high about men.

## CONSIDER YOURSELF FAIRLY WARNED

*We love because it's the only true adventure.*

—NIKKI GIOVANNI

Perhaps you know just by looking at him if there's any shot of a future with a particular man, but I warn you: You just might fall in love with someone you never thought you would.

That's what happened to Amy, who wasn't attracted to Carl at first. Amy was guarded because she was still recovering from a recent breakup. She also decided that Carl wasn't her type because he was balding and stocky. Carl, however, doggedly pursued her after they met on a ski trip. She agreed to go out with him but was so defended it took a long time for her to notice how sweet and smart Carl was.

Carl finally stopped asking when she accidentally stood him up after he'd packed a picnic lunch—complete with homemade beer—for the two of them. When he stopped calling, Amy realized that she missed his warmth, his strength, and the companionship that came with his caring about her so much. That's when Amy decided to call him and offer to take him to a concert she knew he would like.

Carl and Amy are married now with a daughter, and Amy is still deeply in love with her wonderful husband. How did all of this come about? Amy decided to go on a date with a man she wasn't attracted to, which wasn't easy for her. "I would start to feel myself freak out because I was afraid I would disappoint him, so I'd remind myself that it was just a date," she told me. "Then Carl had the chance to win me over—and he succeeded."

This is just one story of a woman falling for a man she wasn't initially excited about. That happens all the time, which is one more reason to let go of your ideas about when, how, and who you'll fall in love with.

If you think you could never fall in love with someone you weren't attracted to right off the bat, consider yourself fairly warned.

## The One Reason to Say No

Feeling unsafe is an important reason to turn down a date. Even if all you have is a vague nagging fear, do not put yourself at risk by going somewhere alone with a man you mistrust for any reason. Heed the part of you that's warning you to be cautious. While you could meet in a public place, you would also be just as wise to say no. Not wanting to hurt someone's feelings is not worth putting yourself in danger. Even if you've already agreed to go, this is one situation where it's acceptable and important to change your mind.

In his book *The Gift of Fear,* Gavin de Becker talks about how a gnawing, uneasy feeling will always have a factual basis. For instance, a man who insists on helping you with your groceries or buying you a drink when you've already said no might set off alarms in your gut, even though on the surface it appears he's just trying to be a gentleman. Your gut may be telling you that this man doesn't take no for an answer, which means you certainly aren't safe with him. Of course, some men will be persistent, which doesn't mean that they're dangerous. So how do you tell the difference? A persistent but safe man will not try to force his suggestions. If you've already said you don't want a drink, for instance, he may try to strike up a conversation, but he won't keep pushing the drink.

De Becker says that every crime has a warning and that you can avoid victimization by trusting the phenomenon of "knowing without knowing why."

Since you trust your instinct to guide you perhaps more than ever before, there's nothing wrong with letting it tell you when to walk away. If that's what your gut is telling you, do it with confidence.

13

# DECLINE DATES WITH DIGNITY

*My good intentions are completely lethal.*

—Margaret Eleanor Atwood

***When you receive an invitation for a second date from a man you aren't interested in, or you need to end a budding relationship, simply say, "I'm sorry, but I'm not available anymore."***

***The only way to avoid disappointing some of the men you date is either to stop dating altogether or to continue dating men you're not interested in. Since neither of those will make you available to the man who's right for you, give yourself permission to disappoint people when necessary. Be sure, however, that you do it in a way that's clear, respectful, and leaves you both with your dignity.***

## Make Sure You Can Swim Before You Jump into the Dating Pool

If you're not sure how to put the brakes on a relationship that seems like it's only going to drain you, you will end up being unavailable to the right man—or worse, you might be inclined to avoid dating altogether. But jumping into the pool isn't so terrifying if you have faith in your ability to swim to the side and get out.

Fortunately, even if you go on dates with lots of men, you won't actually have to decline a second date from most of them. They usually take their cues from you. If it's clear you had a great time and would accept another date, they'll ask again. If they sense that you weren't all that enthusiastic, they probably won't risk rejection by asking you out again. In that case, there's no need to call and tell someone that you won't be going out with him.

However, if you do get an invitation from a man you don't want to date, simply say, "I'm sorry, but I'm not available anymore." No further explanation is necessary. If he asks you why or asks if you're seeing someone else, repeat the words "I'm just not available."

He'll get it.

## Sometimes Being Polite Means Being Elusive

> *One of the lessons of history is that nothing is often a good thing to do and always a clever thing to say.*
>
> —Will Durant

Sometimes women resist saying that they're unavailable because they think it sounds cold or cruel. They think it's "nicer" to say that they have a boyfriend or that they're too busy with work or school. However, your phantom steady could scare away potential suitors if word gets around. What's more, you're compromising yourself in the process of trying to control the man's feelings or reactions. Lying chips away at your integrity and hurts your spirit, so it's not a good option for a Surrendered Single.

As with all surrendering, saying that you're not available is just sticking to what's true for you rather than criticizing, complaining, or insulting him. One woman's standard line was "I don't think this is going to work out," which she said felt less harsh. But the underlying message that men take away from that phrase is that *they* are not workable, which isn't a good feeling. When you say that you're not available, you're not putting yourself down by suggesting that the guy's better off anyway. You're not assuming all responsibility for things not working out by telling him, "It's not you—it's me." You're not blaming him by confiding and saying, "You're just not my type." And you're not putting him off indefinitely by making the see-through excuse "I'm just so busy right now." Since you don't have room in your life for ex-suitors as friends, you definitely won't want to say "Let's just be friends."

Saying that you're not available doesn't put anyone down, nor does it obligate you to a specific course of action. It could mean that you are leaving the country, seeing someone else seriously, becoming a nun, or that you're simply not interested. Whether he chooses to speculate about the specific reason you're unavailable is not your concern.

Your concern is having enough space in your life for the right man to come into it and to treat you the way you've always wanted to be treated. Saying "I'm not available" is an honest way to communicate that you don't want to be involved with him. Moving beyond the *wrong* man is an important part of keeping an opening in your life for the right man.

You might argue that someone you've been seeing for weeks or months deserves more of an explanation than just hearing that you're not available. You may feel that you "owe" him a reason. However, there's no polite way to tell him what you think is wrong with him. If you go down that road, you'll both be worse off. He will be hurt and angry, and you'll have a hangover from having said things that were ultimately unkind. It's nicer to be clear that you won't be going out with him anymore without being specific about why. It's not your job to improve him for the next woman he dates; few people make changes because someone—particularly someone who rejected them—points out their faults.

For instance, if he calls to ask you out on Friday, you would let him know you're unavailable by saying "I don't think so" or simply "no." If he persists, you could simply say "I'm just not available anymore." If he inquires again, let him know that you'd like to leave it at that.

You might think he would demand more of an explanation, but most people don't want to set themselves up to be chastised, which is what he will be asking for if he pushes it. Therefore, a short conversation that makes him aware that you're not available is sufficient. What's more, he probably won't be shocked, since your manner when you were last together would have tipped him off that all was not well.

As you can tell by this example, breaking up over the phone is perfectly acceptable. However, you would want to wait until he contacts you to go out before you tell him that you're no longer available. There's no point in telling someone who hasn't asked that you're not going to date him anymore.

## Declining Dates Is Different from Breaking Hearts

> *Don't let what you cannot do interfere with what you can do.*
>
> —John R. Wooden

Let's say you decide to run an ad for a computer specialist at your company and dozens of people send in their résumés. Next, you interview a half-dozen people and from that group you cull the one person you think would be the best for the job. Since you have only one job to fill, you have no choice but to reject several people who dressed up and came to an interview and the dozens of others who applied. Although you know they may be disappointed, you accept that this is an unavoidable part of the process.

In the same way, having to disappoint men who would like to be with you is part of the process of dating. If you're worried about breaking hearts right and left by accepting every opportunity to date and going out with men who don't seem promising to you, remember that you and your date are grown-ups. Both of you come to the table knowing that there were no guarantees, that in dating there's an implicit risk of heartbreak. Both of you invested the hope that you would benefit. He's just as aware as you are that dating sometimes leaves one person disappointed.

It's no fun to let someone down, but doing so cleanly and with integrity—without lying or dragging out a going-nowhere conversation—is a necessary part of keeping yourself open. It's also part of being a self-respecting adult.

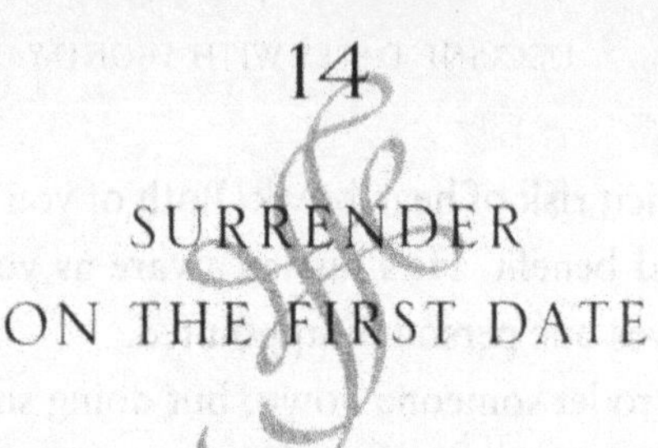

# 14

# SURRENDER ON THE FIRST DATE

*Drawing on my fine command of language, I said nothing.*
—ANONYMOUS

*On a first date surrender your desire to control the flow of the evening. Instead, focus on two missions:*

- *Be quiet—let him do most of the talking—so that you can focus on how you feel and what you want.*
- *Set the stage for the rest of your relationship by letting him know what you expect.*

*These missions might sound contradictory, but they're not.*

## All Quiet on the Dating Front

Like most women, I'm a good talker. Words come easily and I sometimes use them either to fill up long pauses or try to seem more confident.

I was especially talkative on dates. Even when I wasn't trying to calm my nerves or fill up all the pauses, I was trying to impress the guy with my sparkling conversation. I realized, however, that my way of doing things—chattering nervously—simply wasn't working. I wasn't getting asked on second dates, and after each first date, I would spend the next few days feeling bad about the ridiculous things I had said.

If anything, my nervous babbling made the men tune me out or check their watches. I told myself they couldn't handle a smart woman with independent opinions and ideas. In reality, I was sending those men the unappealing signal that I was in control: I was communicating that I knew a lot, was so funny that I deserved extra airtime, and had a repertoire of stories that would impress even the president of the United States. Trying to control the conversation by making sure there was no empty air may have made me feel less nervous, but it also made me less attractive, even to myself.

I was particularly nervous about my first date with John because I was exceptionally attracted to him. I asked my therapist very plainly what I could do *not* to repel him immediately. She suggested that I be quiet during the date.

At first her suggestion sounded nutty to me. What if he thought I was dull? What if he wasn't talkative and felt overburdened having to make all the conversation? How could he get to know me if I didn't tell him all about myself? The therapist pointed out that I would be in a better position to make up my mind about how *I* liked him if I focused on how I felt when I was with him, rather than what I would say next. I resolved to do my best to be quiet.

The night of the date I was more nervous than ever, knowing that I would not have my familiar defense against the awkward moments: talking. "You can be quiet," I told myself throughout the evening, starting when John came to the door. Normally, I would have commented on something banal—the weather, what I knew about where we were going, how excited I was to see *The Philadelphia Story* onstage. Instead, I let him tell me about himself and ask me questions about myself.

Early in the evening, John told me that he was eternally grateful that someone had invented contact lenses, because his glasses looked like two Hubble space telescopes welded together. He went on to say that he sometimes amused himself by looking at the world without correcting his vision. "You can see all kinds of unusual things that way," he said wryly. "Like the devil."

Not only did I laugh at his self-deprecating humor, I relaxed when I realized he was willing to make jokes at his own expense to amuse me. I was grateful. Near the end of the night, I listened to what he thought about the play, smiling all the while and marveling that he could keep up a conversation when I was practically a mute.

In truth, I wasn't a mute at all. I was listening, responding, and talking some—just not as much as I usually would. I was a receptive listener—nodding in understanding, making eye contact, and smiling when I felt amused or happy—and by virtue of that alone, a good conversationalist. For the first time since I'd started dating, I was aware of how I felt with my date. I was noticing what kind of person he was—easygoing, unassuming, playful—instead of thinking of what I would say next. I'd been able to stay more grounded and present than I would have if I'd been jabbering. I had enjoyed myself without trying to keep the conversation hopping. I was even making mental notes to myself, like "nice eyes" and "seems bright."

If I had been my unadulterated, chatty self, I don't know that my mellow, slightly shy husband would have had the opportunity to entertain me that first night. I certainly wouldn't have been able to demonstrate my enjoyment with laughter. The whole date set a precedent for how we behave together to this day: He makes me laugh, and I delight in his sense of humor.

Much later, he told me that he enjoyed that date because he could see I was having a good time. "You seemed happy," he told me, "and I figured I was partly responsible for that." When I was sitting there smiling at him without saying anything, he thought to himself, *She thinks I'm cool.* Apparently, he didn't mind my quietness at all.

So even though I didn't say much, John knew I accepted him, and that meant more to him than if I had been the most impressive conversationalist who ever lived.

## He's the One Who's Auditioning

> *A good listener is not only popular everywhere, but after a while he gets to know something.*
>
> —Wilson Mizner

Refraining from overtalking helped me stay calm and focused on how I felt and what I wanted. I was myself but a more reserved version of myself. Without realizing it, I'd put myself squarely in the position to receive. This probably seemed feminine to John and may have a lot to do with why we hit it off so well on the night of March 18, 1988.

I call this quiet approach surrendered dating. By not trying to control the direction or tone of the conversation, I could hear my own voice more clearly.

The benefit of surrendering on a date is that it allows the woman to be more:

- *observant:* The better we listen and watch, the more information we'll have to help us decide whether to continue dating a guy.
- *confident:* We seem relaxed and at ease when we're not bursting at the seams with something to say.
- *feminine:* We're softer when we're simply smiling and responding than we would be if we were trying to direct the conversation.
- *receptive:* We're better listeners when we're quiet.

Your smile conveys the trusting, positive expectation that your date is up to the task of showing you a good time without your help. Encouraging and empowering him in this way is all you need to do for him to enjoy your company.

I had spent so much time trying to impress men and acting and saying things so that they would like me that I would forget to ask myself how I felt when I was with them or even if I was attracted to them. I put myself in the one-down position, as though I were auditioning and he had all the power to give me the "part" of his girlfriend. Surrendered dating allowed me to gather the information I needed to decide if the man was right for me and set a foundation for the kind of long-term relationship I wanted anyway.

## SURRENDERED MINGLING

Renee complained that she felt overlooked whenever she went to clubs with her girlfriend Mary. "Mary's so flirty and always waving to guys," she said. "Of course, they're all interested in her because she's posing and smiling and playing with her hair. But I don't want to have to act like a ditz, for one thing, and it's embarrassing to seem like I'm on the hunt. I just want them to come to me, but I'm afraid they won't unless I tap dance or something."

But Renee needn't have worried. Ron approached her at a party while she was enjoying herself and talking with friends. She probably looked relaxed and happy as she laughed with them. Ron managed to get her number before the night was through. "I didn't know what to say to him, so I used the surrendered approach by being pretty quiet. I didn't try to fill in the spaces or say anything just to hear myself talk," she reported. As it turned out, Ron had plenty to say and kept her engaged in the conversation by asking her questions. "I wasn't on the prowl at all," Renee remarked. "But he noticed me anyway. And then we hit it off."

Just as you don't have to prove yourself on a date, you can also relax and let the man do the talking when you meet someone at a wedding, party, group hike, or club. Even in a group situation, your powers of attraction will serve you better than an aggressive campaign to get noticed. Your ability to receive, listen, and stay grounded will give you more power than your best effort to impress a man.

## USE THE DISTRESS TEST

> *The woman who survives in tact and happy must be at once tender and tough. She must have convinced herself . . . that she, her values, and her choices are important.*
>
> —MAYA ANGELOU

Just because you're not saying much on the first date doesn't mean that you will be acquiescing to his whims. Part of the reason for being quiet is to focus on what you want and how you feel. So the more you listen to your heart messages, the easier it will be to honor your feelings and desires by expressing them at the right time.

There are two instances when it is appropriate and important that you communicate with your date about your feelings and desires:

- He's asked you for your preference (e.g., would you rather go to a disco or a jazz club?).
- He's suggesting the two of you do something that will put you in emotional or physical distress (e.g., he's planning to take you to a horror film that will give you nightmares for weeks, or on a hike through pollens that will set off your allergies).

Whenever your date asks you what you would like, whether it's which ice cream flavor you prefer or whether to put the top down in the car, he is considering your comfort and needs your input. There's no benefit to staying quiet in this instance. Simply say what you prefer. Even if he's already said he likes to have the top down, it's fair to tell him that you prefer the top up when he asks. A good guy wants to know what will make you happy more than he wants to have things his way.

Speaking up about your preferences won't make you any less gracious or feminine, just more comfortable and present. No one who hopes to please and impress you would want to put you through something that would hurt you. Therefore, if a man you're with suggests anything that would put you in distress, simply say no.

Notice the difference, however, between something that will distress you emotionally or physically and something that just isn't your favorite. For instance, let's say your date wants to take you to an eighteenth-century poetry reading and you suspect it will be boring. Unless he gives you another option (e.g., the sitar concert or a cruise around the harbor) consider broadening your horizons a bit by attending the reading amiably. After all, it won't hurt you.

The idea is to speak up to prevent yourself from being in a situation that will cause you real emotional or physical distress. Outside of that, hold your tongue and go along for the adventure.

## Kiss on the First Date

> *A very small degree of hope is sufficient to cause the birth of love.*
>
> —Stendhal

Maybe you've heard that it's better to be friends with a man before you start dating him. Maybe you think that letting him kiss you on the first date will make him think you're easy or impair your judgment about him. Maybe you're afraid that once you start kissing him you will go too far.

Kissing is not nearly as dangerous as you think.

Naturally, there's nothing wrong with starting to date a man with whom you are already friends, but there's also nothing wrong with going directly into a romantic relationship with a man you just met.

Remember that the tone of the first date goes a long way toward setting the tone of the entire relationship. If you offer him a friendly handshake or a hug, you're signaling that you're not interested in him romantically. Refusing a kiss from a man you are attracted to also means denying yourself the pleasure and fun of making out, and why do that?

Remember: ***If you want a romantic relationship with your date, let him kiss you.***

Kissing doesn't prevent you from getting to know someone. Having sex with someone right away could put a relationship into fifth gear and impair your judgment about him, but kissing has no such power. A kiss might make you giddy, but it doesn't have the same mind-altering effect as sex. You can kiss a guy for an hour on the first date—as long as it's just kissing—without fear of being too easy. A make-out session will only leave him wanting more and motivate him to call you again for another date.

Maybe you worry that you're too weak-willed to avoid having sex with him if you let him kiss you. If at the end of the date you invite him in and take him straight to the bedroom then, yes, it will be tough to stick to straight kissing. But if you let him kiss you in a public place, like at a restaurant or in front of the door to your house or apartment building, then kissing can remain innocent. The way to orchestrate a temptation-free kiss is to stay in public by saying good-night from your front door.

## Take Off Your Running Shoes

When you get to your front door, if he hasn't kissed you yet and you wish he would, then stand there and look at him. This is where it's tempting to chatter or just run inside, but you're more likely to get what you want by standing still to give him ample opportunity to lean over and touch your lips with his. I know it's not easy, but it is necessary if you want a tender good-night kiss. If you get a peck when you were hoping for a smooch, you'll feel some momentary rejection, but any guy who doesn't take advantage of some hot lips when he sees them is a waste of your time anyway.

Jana had a very tough time with this. She was often so nervous anticipating a kiss that she ran inside without giving the guy a chance to kiss her, even when she wanted to be kissed. "Well, bye!" she would call from inside the doorway, having suddenly scampered up a whole flight of stairs ahead of her date. If you're not letting yourself enjoy good-night kisses, take a tip from Jana and take off your running shoes. Start accepting kisses, and your chances of finding someone you like to kiss will improve immeasurably.

## Ending Dates Without Guilt

Rita's date was rude and self-absorbed. By the time dinner was over, she wanted to go home. Instead, she lingered with him in some shops near the restaurant to be polite. "He'd driven such a long way," she explained. "I didn't want to just end the evening after dinner. It seemed rude."

But ending a date when you're ready isn't impolite. It spares you both the pain of having to make small talk when it's clear there's no hope of a romance blossoming, and it's good self-care.

If your date is rude or crude and you don't want to linger, you're under no obligation to stay. If he asks you what you want to do next, you can say, "I'm ready to go home now." If he doesn't ask, you can offer that you're ready to go home.

Simply saying what you want is not an insult or a criticism. You don't have to stay longer because he drove a long way, spent a lot on dinner, or says he really likes you. If it's not a match, there's no reason to drag out the date.

## Let Him Know What You Expect

> *You have to walk carefully in the beginning of love; the running across fields into your lover's arms can only come later when you're sure they won't laugh if you trip.*
>
> —Jonathan Carroll

Now that you're clear on how you'll conduct yourself on the first date, the only problem is getting him to hold up his end of the bargain, which, of course, you can't control. As with all surrendering, you can't dictate how he behaves—only how you react to him.

You can, however, let him know what you expect from him in terms of treating you like a woman. In most cases, guiding him won't be necessary. As much as women have changed socially over the last forty years, most men approach dating the same way they have always approached it: by asking a woman out, picking her up, paying her way, considering her comfort, and seeing her home.

However, you may encounter a man who, instead of offering to pick you up, suggests that you meet him somewhere. Should that happen, the following phrase will be very useful: "I prefer to be picked up."

Of course, if you're meeting a man from a dating service and you're not comfortable telling him where you live, it's okay to agree to meet him someplace. But as long as you feel safe enough to give him your address, let him know you prefer to be picked up.

There's no need to explain or justify your preference. You're simply letting him know what will work for you. He then has the option of doing what you prefer. Again, the reason for doing this is to let him know how you like to be treated and to set the tone for romance from the very beginning. A man who offers to pick you up will play the role of protector and provider throughout the date. (This is true even if you had to prompt him to come get you.)

If a prospective date expresses hesitation about picking you up, or starts to debate about whether it's reasonable or practical, then say, "If you can't come by tonight, maybe we should reschedule for another night." If he wants to see you, he will gladly come and get you, even if it's an hour's drive, even if he has to walk in the rain, even if it's out of his way.

*Wait a minute. Didn't you say that I should go out with any man who asks me as long as he doesn't have two heads?*

I did say that, but I'm making an important exception. A man who is not willing to go out of his way to come and get you on the first date is not the right man for you. He has forgotten what it means to be a man, to feel the pride of symbolically taking care of a woman. Perhaps such a man will get reacquainted with his masculinity someday, but there's no sense in waiting for that when the man who's right for you is waiting to meet you right now.

Bonnie learned this the hard way. She was looking forward to going out with Perry, who had invited her to dinner and a movie. The day of the date, he asked her if she would mind swinging by his place so they could leave from there. Bonnie agreed to come over after dropping her daughter off at the sitter.

When she got to Perry's house, his eyes were bloodshot and he seemed distant. He had ordered in Chinese food, so Bonnie felt she had no choice but to eat at his house. They had barely finished eating when he fell asleep on the couch. Bonnie watched the end of a Beatles special while he snored, then showed herself out, terribly disappointed.

Perry is the kind of guy who probably would not have come to get Bonnie no matter what she said she preferred. If she'd let him know that she didn't think it was going to work out because of that, she would have saved herself the disappointment of spending an evening with a man who was unappealing and probably stoned.

Any man you go out with is incredibly lucky that you agreed to spend the evening with him. You might have chosen to spend time with friends or a good book, but instead, you let him enjoy your pleasant smiling face and your congenial company. If you hadn't, he wouldn't be feeling proud and fortunate for the opportunity to please you and win you over. He wouldn't feel as masculine and needed if he didn't have the privilege of picking you up, opening your doors, paying the bill, driving you around, and showing you home again.

If you keep that perspective, chances are he will, too.

# 15

# MAKE ALL OF YOUR DATES FUN

*Laughter is the closest distance between two people.*

—VICTOR BORGE

***In a survey of thousands of men, all of them said that when they take a woman out they want her to be happy—and he will be looking for feedback that you are enjoying yourself.***

***So if you want your date to lead to lasting romance, the first step is to let your suitor know that he is successful in his mission to make you happy.***

***Make having a good time your first priority on a date. If you've been feeling stressed out and think relaxing is only for retirement, it's time to reacquaint yourself with the feeling of being carefree and fun-loving.***

## Become the Goddess of Fun and Light

The Goddess of Fun and Light is quick to laugh and loves to play. Never stodgy or serious, she is happy and vivacious. Others are drawn to her because she smiles and invites conversation. The men she dates always feel successful because she enjoys herself so much when she's out with them. In fact, they'd like to be with her more because her good mood is infectious.

The Goddess of Fun and Light isn't dancing on the tables or constantly cracking jokes, but she remembers how to be carefree. The Goddess of Fun and Light never forgets that men take her out for her enjoyment; she trusts that the man she is with wants everything that happens during the evening to delight her. She enjoys sensual pleasures—tasting the food, listening to music, feeling the sand between her toes. She doesn't worry about impressing anyone or saying the right thing, because that wouldn't be fun. The Goddess can be sophisticated and gorgeous, smart and sultry, but above all she finds pleasure in her situation, because that's what makes her feel great—and him feel successful.

If your goal on a date is to impress him or to find a husband, you're trying to control his impression of you or make him into someone who might not even be right. Sure, you want to meet someone with whom you'll have a romantic relationship, but the goal of a date is to have fun. Only fun dates lead to lasting love. If you have fun, you'll want to see someone again. And that will lead to getting to know him better, which, in turn, leads to a deeper relationship.

## Look for Fun in All the Right Places

So how can you be the Goddess of Fun and Light?

Avoid complaining.

If your date takes you to the movies on the film's opening night and the line is around the block, you can see it as an adventure and an opportunity to see how he handles the ensuing conversation time instead of commenting on the long wait. If he takes you river rafting and you end up soaking wet, you can turn the occasion into a flirtatious splash fest instead of having a fit. If he's playing Garth Brooks in the car and you hate Garth Brooks but love country music, you can say, "You like country music too?" instead of "I can't stand this egotistical jerk!"

The Goddess states her needs, but she is always gracious. For instance, if you were cold, you'd say so. If you were hungry, tired, or wanted a break from an activity, you'd speak up in a direct way without criticizing your companion's choices, judgment, or his own sense of fun. So you would say, "I'm cold," not "Don't you think it's just a tad ridiculous to be outside in this weather?" "It's getting awfully late to eat dinner," becomes "Gee, I'm hungry." See the difference? The first phrase criticizes his judgment and is an attempt to control the flow of the date, while the second just states the facts. If you insult the activity or the food, he may take it personally because you're putting down his choice. So instead of saying, "This is boring," "I've done this before," or "This food is awful," find the entertainment in your situation and focus on that.

The Goddess would never insult her date. Whether she finds him charming or revolting, she's going to be with him for only a few hours. If she doesn't enjoy his company, she won't go out with him again, but there's no reason to pummel his self-esteem in the meantime. And there's every reason to look for fun in the situation—whether it's trying food you've never tasted, going someplace new, or just catching the latest movie. The goal is to enjoy yourself as much as possible.

The Goddess of Fun and Light is:

- *agreeable:* She says "yes" to everything, unless she feels it will put her in emotional or physical distress.
- *smart:* But she knows she doesn't have to prove it. She doesn't dumb down while she's out with a man, but she doesn't engage in petty arguments just to prove that she's right. That wouldn't be fun.
- *relaxed:* She doesn't check her watch or remind her date they better hurry if they're going to make it to the movie on time. She trusts that her date can take care of those details. She knows better than to try to control the flow of the evening.
- *pleasant:* Even if she had a rotten day at work, the Goddess is ready to leave behind daily hassles and stresses and have a good time.
- *optimistic:* She always expects that things will go well, because she knows it improves her chances that they will.
- *surrendered:* She never tells her date what to do or how to do it. She doesn't want to set up a controlling pattern.
- *self-respecting:* The Goddess doesn't put herself down even to be modest. After all, she is a goddess.

## How to be Humble Without Being Modest

*The most terrifying thing is to accept oneself completely.*
—Carl Jung

There are two reasons that we try to be modest:

1. *Because we're soliciting a compliment—otherwise known as trying to control what the other person will say.* Comments like "I'm so fat!" or "I'm a terrible dancer" are really veiled pleas for a compliment or reassurance. You hope that someone else will say, "Oh no—you've got a great body," or "You dance beautifully." So, rather than being humble, you've advertised your insecurity and asked people to respond to it, which is self-centered and controlling.
2. *Out of fear.* Once, on a date with a friend of a friend, I decided to reveal all my defects right away so as not to prolong a relationship that I was afraid would fall apart anyway. I actually said to him, "I have a big problem with credit cards. Even though I have a huge debt already, I keep using them and getting myself into a worse hole, and now creditors are calling." Not only was this not a light, fun conversation, but this comment made me about as charming as if I'd worn a Sherman button to a Georgia picnic.

I did have a problem with credit cards at that time, but I made this detrimental confession to someone I barely knew, not because I was humble but because I was afraid. I was much more than just my credit card debt. I was also a top student with an infectious laugh and a knack for making great vegetarian lasagna. But I neglected to mention those things on this particular date because I was trying to be "humble."

Modesty is about rejecting your own gifts. Dismissing my blessings wasn't endearing—it was disingenuous. Modesty leaves those around you with the burden of having to reassure you or point out those gifts that you're dismissing. When someone puts herself down, your first reaction is to contradict her, to tell her that her garden really is lovely, that she's not at all stupid. Everyone makes mistakes, dinner was excellent, and what do you mean you're not a good cook?

Those conversations take a lot of energy. They're boring and stiff, too.

Not fun.

To be humble, you must first be truthful, and when you are truthful, you must also be grateful. We've been conditioned to believe that being humble means professing unworthiness. I know it sounds like a contradiction to say that humility without gratitude is deceit, but thinking you're unworthy is actually a lie. It's appropriate to appreciate your gifts.

This self-respecting approach encourages others to treat you well, while talking poorly about yourself could cause those around you—including romantic prospects—to value you less. After all, if we're always talking about our deficiencies and faults, that's what they're likely to see in us too.

## Humility Comes from Within

*I may not be totally perfect, but parts of me are excellent.*
—Ashleigh Brilliant

Think of humility, rather than false modesty, as the goal. In order to have humility, you must first identify and appreciate your own gifts.

Recognize that while you are certainly not perfect or better than someone else, you are fortunate in many ways. Humility means understanding that you have lots of goodness and even moments of greatness in you, and that others do, too. You realize that the world is full of gifted people, and that you are only one of them. Knowing that there are others who can sew better, throw a ball faster, or sing higher than you doesn't make you inadequate, but it keeps you humble. Recognizing your limitations—not pretending you're unworthy—is a beautiful and attractive quality.

Maya Angelou said: "Modesty is a learned affectation . . . that speaks volumes about falseness. Humility comes from within." Having humility means that you keep your gifts in perspective. Being modest means that you pretend you don't have any gifts to begin with, which is just as offensive as pretending that you have omnipotence.

So how did I tell John about my problems with credit cards? I didn't have to. Shortly after we started dating he was at my apartment when a collector called, and he overheard the conversation. I burned with embarrassment, but an amazing thing happened: John didn't like me any less after that. Maybe it was because he had already tasted my lasagna or because he enjoyed my hearty laugh. He had already gotten to know the real me, and he saw enough positive things to stick around.

## Being Who You Originally Were

*Be what nature intended you for, and you will succeed; be anything else, and you will be ten thousand times worse than nothing.*

—Sydney Smith

You might argue that you can't do the things suggested in this chapter because it's not who you are to be the Goddess of Fun and Light or to talk about your gifts instead of your faults. Maybe you're more prone to being serious and cynical. Maybe you think life is full of hard work and that being playful is superficial.

If you don't feel like the Goddess of Fun and Light, maybe you're just out of practice. Maybe the light and fun are buried under layers of discouragement, disappointment, and defense. But that's not who you are. If you dig a little deeper, you'll unearth an authentic part of you that loves to frolic, dream, and dance. Yes, you have responsibilities, and things don't always go your way, but you still love a good time when the opportunity presents itself.

Perhaps being playful and laughing often *is* your true nature. After all, that's how most of us start out in life, and it surely feels better to laugh than it does to worry. You weren't put on the planet to be serious all the time.

If nothing else, just reading this book is proof of your optimism. You wouldn't have bothered if you didn't have hope that you could improve your happiness by letting love into it. That alone will help you find the fun and light inside of you.

# 16

# KEEP FLIRTING WITH EVERY GUY YOU SEE

*It is a mistake to look too far ahead. Only one link in the chain of destiny can be handled at a time.*

—Sir Winston Churchill

***Even if you think the guy you went out with last weekend is a dream, don't stop flirting with every guy you see. Flirting distracts you from focusing on one person and helps you resist the urge to call him, put yourself in his path, or otherwise control his pursuit. Having other offers keeps your options open and gives you something to think about besides when he's going to call again.***

## Give Me Patience Now!

Kelly fell hard for James. She spent almost a week after their first date trying to will the phone to ring, but it didn't. By midweek her anticipation turned to anger and disappointment that he wasn't pursuing her as quickly as she wanted to be pursued.

She wanted to make him call somehow, but of course she couldn't. Instead, she focused on other things. Luckily, she had a date lined up with Ted and a heavy flirtation going with a coworker, which were great distractions. By the time James did call, three full weeks later, it was just a pleasant surprise—not the equivalent of administering CPR to someone who's had a heart attack.

It turned out James had been traveling for work most of those three weeks. He was calling to ask if she would go to a movie with him.

## Accept That Acceptance Is Your Only Choice

> *We cannot conquer fate and necessity, yet we can yield to them in such a manner as to be greater than if we could.*
>
> —Walter Savage Landor

Of course, what Kelly wanted was to control—somehow, someway—when James would call. Needless to say, there was nothing she could do to make him call. Even leaving him messages, trying to bump into him, and passing notes through a friend couldn't make her phone ring. And if she caved in to her desire to control him, not only would she appear desperate, she'd also be doing the pursuing and cheating herself out of the joy of being pursued.

As a Surrendered Single, she had only one choice: accept.

That's the challenge: staying surrendered. Having the attention of other men helped Kelly meet that challenge. She used the energy she once would have put into obsessing, fuming, or making a rash decision, into enjoying herself with other men. She still thought about James, and she wasn't nearly as interested in Ted or her coworker as she was in him. Still, she kept herself open to other prospects—and saw some—and that helped keep her relaxed and cheered.

What could be more appealing to a suitor and healthier for your outlook?

Letting James become her whole universe after only one or two dates—no matter how well they went—would have undermined Kelly's self-esteem and peace of mind. The minute you let yourself start thinking, *Why hasn't he called? Was it something I said?* you're trying to find a way to control when he calls and what he thinks of you. If you find yourself wondering about something you *think* you *maybe* shouldn't have said, you're using your energy to make yourself crazy. Worse still, if you act on this impulse, chances are good that you'll destroy what you're trying to fix. You simply can't control another's actions, reactions, or plans.

Feeling sorry for yourself—or worse, criticizing yourself—when someone doesn't call only makes you feel terrible. That self-doubt then robs you of the energy you need to flirt with every man you see so you can keep your options open.

Don't rope yourself into focusing on a single man until you're in a committed relationship with him. Just as you wouldn't take your house off of the market until you had a firm offer in hand, don't decline dates or stop flirting with other men because you're particularly interested in one.

With this philosophy in mind, Ellen agreed to go out with Jason even though she was more excited about her budding relationship with Paul. She panicked when she ran into a friend of Paul's at a restaurant while she was out with Jason. She was worried that Paul would lose interest if he found out she was dating other men. Instead, when Paul saw her the next day, he asked her how she had enjoyed eating at the restaurant where his friend had spotted her. Then he teased her: "You see that? I'm keeping tabs on you."

Finding out that she went on a date with someone else didn't diminish Paul's attraction to Ellen one iota. In fact, learning that she had other suitors piqued his interest, the same way seeing someone else grab a dress that you were eyeing makes you wish you had bought it while you had the chance.

## Agonizing Is Not a Good Hobby

Going out with Jason was an enjoyable diversion for Ellen. She got out of the house, had a nice dinner, and basked in his admiration, which boosted her self-esteem. And who knows? When Paul saw her the next day, he might even have picked up on her confidence, and *that* alone could have made her more attractive to him. As nice as that is, continuing to flirt and date men while you're hoping to get to know another man better is *not* about hoping he'll find out and want you more. That would be trying to manipulate the situation. Rather, it's about living a rich life and staying in the market until you're not in the market anymore.

Continuing to flirt will help the man who is right for you recognize you when he sees you. You may think you're with him already, but stay open to the possibilities, just in case. The femininity that comes with flirting—and the positive feedback it elicits—will also help you feel good about yourself. Most of all, it will prevent you from agonizing needlessly over whether a man you barely know will be in your future.

# 17

# STAY IN THE MOMENT

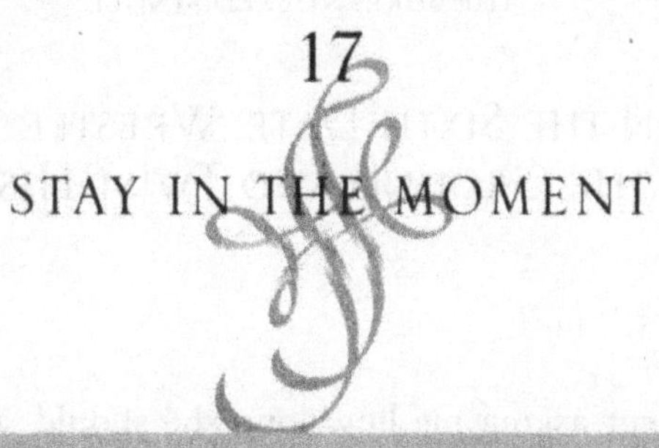

*An adventure is only an inconvenience rightly considered. An inconvenience is only an adventure wrongly considered.*

—G. K. CHESTERTON

*Avoid holding a state of the union address.*

*Honor your desires but let the relationship unfold naturally and take its course without trying to manipulate it.*

*The instant you find yourself casually asking him about things like whether he thinks a woman should stay at home with the children while the husband supports the family, you're not in a relationship anymore. You're in a fantasy about your future that has nothing to do with the man in front of you. By eliciting his response, you're trying to control where the relationship is going.*

*Instead of trying to control your date or new beau to be the kind of man you want him to be, stay focused on your own feelings and desires and enjoy the moment.*

## On the Sixth Date, Wrestle Him to the Ground and Twist His Arm

Dana kept asking me how long she should wait before discussing some important issues with Patrick, such as how often they would be seeing each other, when their relationship would become exclusive, and whether he planned to get married. She was trying to get past that nagging feeling that they might hit a snag somewhere down the road, and the insecurity drove her to want to discuss everything now. I teased her by saying, "On the sixth date, you wrestle him to the ground and twist his arm until he agrees to call you every day and sets a wedding date."

Imagine if, after some certain specified period of time (the moment you realize you want to see him again), you could sit down and hammer out all the details. You could discuss issues such as which holidays you would spend with your in-laws, how many children you'd have of each gender, and whether to retire in Arizona or Florida. Wouldn't that be great?

Perhaps. But it would also make life pretty dull and predictable. Sure, you wouldn't have to be anxious about the future, but you wouldn't be pleasantly surprised either. Just think: If you determine everything at once, you might never take an impromptu walk in the rain to get Indian food or decide to forget the families at the holidays and just run away to a cabin in the mountains. Having to wait for life's plans to reveal themselves is more exciting and uncertain.

We can't predict the future, nor can we exact heartfelt commitments from a man on command. We might like to sometimes, when we're feeling insecure or impatient, but it can't be done. Trying to is simply an effort to control the relationship and a surefire way to drive it into the ground.

# DON'T TRAMPLE A TENDER MOMENT BY RUNNING TO THE NEXT MILESTONE

> *You can't bring back the past, and you're not promised the future, so enjoy life now.*
>
> —KIMO PAKI

You can connect with someone else only in the present, not while you're thinking about the future.

Staying in the moment will also give you an accurate picture of the man you're with. Quizzing him on his intentions is really a way of testing him to see if he measures up to your checklist. That puts undue pressure on him. Giving your date a twenty-point survey early on to make sure that you both hold the same things dear makes him feel invisible. You're trying to fit him into your mold of what you want in a future husband.

In short, you are unconsciously trying to control him to be the man that you want him to be instead of surrendering to the man that he is.

A Surrendered Single makes a point of focusing on and celebrating the present. She hopes for and expects the best, and is grateful for what she's experiencing right now. She knows she can't be anywhere else anyway.

That's not to say that you don't make plans for the future. Staying in the moment doesn't mean that you would date someone for years when what you really want is to get married. Rather, staying present minded means that you savor each stage of the relationship, instead of mentally fast-forwarding to your tenth wedding anniversary.

A Surrendered Single prefers the natural progression of a healthy developing relationship to a forced Vulcan mind meld on the first date. She recognizes that a sweet, solid romance is built over time and that there is no other way to create the blissful union she craves.

## Leave State of the Union Addresses to the President

"But how do I know if there's a future in this relationship?" Dana would ask. "How do I know I'm not wasting my time?"

Unfortunately for Dana and all of us who are like her, you can't possibly know if you're wasting your time. There are things you can do at each step to minimize your risk, but having a state of the union address is not one of them.

A state of the union address is a conversation with an agenda—your agenda. And that is to get him to say what you want to hear about the future: that you'll be married someday, that he is the marrying type, that the two of you will live near your family, etc. The subtext is "I want to know now, before I waste any more time, whether you're going to love me forever or not." The problem is, forcing such a statement renders it meaningless. Since we know this on some level, we often approach state of the union addresses in a covert way, using manipulation to exact a commitment without seeming to force it.

Unfortunately, this never works.

For Heidi, state of the union addresses always took place on her olive green couch when she was feeling insecure and wanted to make sure she wouldn't be abandoned. "I was trying to get him to reassure me that we would always be together, that we had a future," she admits now. "But they were always miserable conversations. I think even the couch was happier when I stopped initiating those kinds of conversations."

Nancy's final state of the union address with her boyfriend Roy wasn't covert at all. After a fight, and in her anger (and fear), she demanded to know right then if he ever intended to marry her. You can guess how he answered this self-defeating inquiry.

Fear is always behind the urge to have a state of the union address. The way to avoid acting on your fear is to abstain from those types of conversations. Instead of trying to coerce him to say certain words when you're feeling anxious, reflect on his actions, which really do speak louder.

Perhaps your insecurity is rooted in your gut, which is telling you that he's losing interest. If he's not calling much, doesn't make plans to get together, or seems less physically affectionate, then your feelings may be an appropriate response to the early signs of a possible breakup.

However, if you're scared that he doesn't like you anymore because he spent an evening with his friends, was quiet during dinner, or didn't answer his cell phone when you called, your fear has more to do with you than with him. This is where a girlfriend who can give you a reality check will come in handy. You're only human, and it's natural to get nervous when the future of the relationship is important to you. However, you're better off getting the reassurance you need somewhere else rather than trying to beat it out of him.

You might argue that it's just as well that Nancy found out when she did that Roy didn't imagine a future with Nancy in it. However, there is still the possibility that her timing in asking the question may have influenced the outcome. Demanding to know his intentions when they were both angry made it difficult, if not impossible, for Roy to respond with tenderness. Perhaps he did love

Nancy enough to marry her, but he wasn't about to admit it under those circumstances.

## Avoid Premature Planning

> *This very moment is a seed from which the flowers of tomorrow's happiness grow.*
>
> — Margaret Lindsey

It's natural to want to make plans for the future. The point is to wait until the moment is right and not to get too far ahead of yourself. Here are some examples of loaded topics that single women sometimes raise prematurely:

***Marriage***

***Sample questions:*** "Do you think you'll ever get married?" "Do your parents pressure you to get married?" "How old would you like to be when you get married?"

***When it's appropriate:*** If you've had only two dates and you're thinking you want to marry the guy, maybe you will. But bringing up marriage before you've been together for at least six months short-changes you of the time you need to make a thoughtful decision. Staying focused on how you feel and what you want will help you be certain about whether committing to him is right for you when the time comes.

After six months of dating, if you want to take the relationship to the next level and he's not making any such moves, you'll need to say so directly. You can also state your desires to have a husband after three months. (I discuss this in detail in chapter 27.) Trying to manipulate him into expressing his desire to marry you is unproductive, unattractive, and dishonest.

*Kids*

***Sample questions:*** "Do you like kids?" "Do you want to have kids some day?" "Would you want your wife to stay home with the kids?"

***When it's appropriate:*** If you ask a man any of these questions before there's been any talk of marriage, you're way ahead of yourself. If he's adamantly opposed to having kids, you'll find out soon enough through ordinary conversation. Otherwise, trying to determine how he feels about children on the second date is not about getting to know him—it's about wanting to predict the outcome of your life.

Only after you're engaged to him do you need to seriously discuss his preferences in relation to children or to tell him yours. Before you get to that, you'd want to make sure that he's someone you want to spend the rest of your life with. Only then can you discuss kids.

If you're freaking out about this suggestion, consider Denise's story. When she asked her new boyfriend Paul how he felt about having kids, he hedged. "I'm not sure if I want them," he told her. Worried that she would never be able to fulfill her dream of being a mother with Paul, Denise broke up with him. Years later, she learned that he was married and the doting father of two boys.

Paul's response to Denise's question reflects an appropriate caution and thoughtfulness about an important decision. As he matured and settled into his marriage, he must have decided that he did want kids. Or maybe he became willing to stretch because he realized it was important to his wife to be a mother.

I'm not suggesting that you marry a man who doesn't want kids and try to change his mind. However, a man who's tentative about having offspring will often overcome his own reluctance and enter into fatherhood to make his wife happy. Therefore, your focus should be on whether he is devoted to you, not on whether his five-, ten-, and twenty-year plans match perfectly with yours. People change. You'll want to find a man you're crazy in love with first and then have kids with him—not look for a father for your unborn children.

The man you marry will be your companion, partner, and lover before you have kids and after your children have grown. He's got to be someone you would want to be with forever even if you never had kids, because he will likely be with you for longer than your children will. Therefore, think of children as a fringe benefit of marriage, not the primary goal.

Your future kids deserve parents who love each other madly. You can give them no greater gift. Therefore, use the time that you're dating to determine whether a man is right for you. Don't lose focus by getting ahead of yourself.

*Money*

***Sample questions or comments:*** "You must do pretty well in your business." "You must make a fortune." "It's tough to make a living in that field." "Is it true that people in your business make six figures?" "I've always wanted to live in (expensive neighborhood). Have you ever thought of moving to (expensive neighborhood)?"

***When it's appropriate:*** Again, you might think this conversation is helping you get to know him better, when really what you're doing is having a fantasy about how rich or how broke you're going to be after you marry this guy. You've left this moment and gone into some fantasy future world. That means you're missing your life right now, including the budding relationship you're in.

Focusing on your date's financial status is also a distraction from observing more important qualities. Money comes and money goes. Is he generous and thoughtful? Does he make you laugh and feel beautiful inside and out? Are you attracted to him?

You will learn all about a man—including his relationship with money—just from being around him while you're dating. Instead of resorting to manipulative questions, focus on how you feel when you're with him and observe his attitude toward money.

Before we met, John went out with a woman who brought brochures for houses in an expensive neighborhood on their second date. She showed them to John excitedly, and he immediately realized that she wasn't interested in him so much as she was the future she had fashioned in her imagination. She was so far ahead of herself that she missed seeing John at all. Because she was so busy imagining their future home, she missed his silly jokes, his compliments, and the pleasure of connecting romantically. She could have just stayed at home with her brochures for all the intimacy they had. He never went out with her again.

*Sex*

***Sample questions and comments:*** "I don't believe in sex before marriage." "I never have sex on the first date."

***When it's appropriate:*** Saying you don't believe in sex before marriage is a reasonable thing to say when you're trying to fend off his advances—not during dinner on the first date before anybody asked.

Vivian made such an announcement early in the hopes that Jared wouldn't try to have sex with her while they were dating.

When she had sex with him anyway she felt foolish and guilty. "I'm wondering how he can ever respect what I say now," she told me.

Although Vivian was sincere in wanting to abstain from sex prior to marriage, she went about it in a way that reflected a lack of commitment. Jared probably didn't put much stock in her out-of-nowhere announcement for the same reason you wouldn't put much credence into a child announcing he is going to be a fireman.

While it's tempting to make blanket statements with words such as "never" and "always" in them, adult relationships are ongoing negotiations. Making a commitment means being willing to make that choice each time the issue arises—not by issuing a single edict. Instead, focus on—you guessed it—how you feel and what you want. Had Vivian been willing to enforce her conviction in the moment that they were about to become sexual, Jared probably would have taken her more seriously.

# 18

# SEPARATE THE GOOD GUYS FROM THE BAD BOYS

*The only tyrant I accept in this world is the still voice within.*

—Mahatma Gandhi

*While you're dating and making assessments of the men you meet, listen to your gut.*

*Your intuition is like the voice of a very shy child who wants to whisper in your ear. You won't be able to hear the message unless you take the time to let her get very close to you and muster up her courage. If something's not right, you'll know it if you listen to yourself.*

*If there's something very right between you and a man, you'll know that, too.*

## The Three Types of Men to Avoid

You can't know immediately if a guy is a heartache waiting to happen. However, you can protect yourself from investing in a doomed relationship by soundly rejecting a man as soon as you discover he is any of the following:

- actively addicted to alcohol, drugs, or gambling;
- physically abusive;
- incapable of being faithful to you.

Maybe you're thinking that this list should be much longer, but in my experience, this is the entire group of men you need to watch out for.

By focusing on whether your date has an addiction, is physically abusive, or incapable of being faithful, you will protect yourself from a myriad of other undesirable behaviors.

## Don't Get Used to Crumbs

*Love is shown in your deeds, not in your words.*

—Fr. Jerome Cummings

One woman described how she looked forward to the instances when her boyfriend became slightly intoxicated, because he seemed more emotionally available. Another woman had been cheated on so many times by one boyfriend that she came to believe that all men were unfaithful and she should get used to it. These women had grown satisfied with eating the crumbs off the floor instead of expecting to be served the feast they deserved.

The man who is right for you will be kind and go out of his way to protect you from harm. He'll tell you silly jokes or sing you sweet songs without needing a drink first. A good guy may admire other women, but he won't touch them once he's committed to you.

There are two dangers of staying in a substandard relationship with one of these bums for even one more minute:

- You'll quickly lose your feelings of self-worth and begin to normalize the awful behavior.
- You'll prevent sweet, decent men from coming into your life. You won't have the energy for them. Plus, a good man may not woo you if he thinks he's invading another guy's territory. The static on your radar will emit an "unavailable" signal to other men.

## He'll Tell You Exactly Who He Is

"But how do I know if there's a future in this relationship?" date him, if a man falls into one of these categories? You may not know in the first few weeks of dating. Sometime within the first month, however, you will get a very accurate sense if you listen to your gut.

Women who are married to addicts, philanderers, and physical abusers often say that they had a feeling well before they were married that something was amiss. For instance, one woman whose husband was unfaithful throughout their twenty-three-year marriage told me that her husband cheated on her—and she knew about it—while they were dating. Another wife told me that her then-boyfriend threw a potted plant at her during a fight only a short time after they started dating. Still another described her husband-to-be as someone who got smashed almost every night just a few weeks after they hooked up.

The red flags were raised. Perhaps these women were afraid of being alone and so decided to ignore the warnings and invest their hearts. Maybe they didn't realize they could never ever change such a man.

The point is that *they knew up front exactly what they were signing up for.*

So will you.

How can I be so sure about this? Because people reveal themselves in everything from the way they walk and what they wear to the food they eat and the music they play. Our vices, friends, hangouts, and habits all say something about us. The man you're dating is no exception. Long before he becomes your mate, there will be clues about exactly who he is and what to expect in the future. In fact, sometimes people will tell you what you need to know about them straight out.

## Your Intuition Isn't Broken

> *Just trust yourself; then you will know how to live.*
>
> —Johann Wolfgang von Goethe

Of course, not every man will be transparent. That's why it's important that you get in the habit of listening to your intuition.

This is particularly true when you're feeling uncertain. If you're wondering whether he gambles too much, but you're not sure, ask your gut. Maybe you didn't think much about the fact that he always carries a deck of cards with him and that he had to pawn his stereo to cover a losing bet on the Super Bowl. However, your intuition has already processed what you know and is sounding the alarm. All you have to do is listen.

You don't even have to know why the alarm is going off, as long as you heed the warning.

Sometimes women will tell me that they fear that their intuition is broken because they've made bad choices in the past. But intuition doesn't break or leave you. Perhaps you haven't listened to it in the past, but it's still there, telling you what's in your best interest.

Intuition is a quiet voice that you hear when you're alone with your thoughts. Perhaps your intuition talks to you while you're out running or folding the laundry. It will come out in your journal and when you meditate. The key is to be quiet. Turn off the radio, television, phone, and other distractions. Wait for the message.

Check in with your stomach. Do you feel anxiety when you think about him? Call a friend for a reality check. If you feel yourself not wanting to tell someone else something you've learned about him, at least have a conversation with yourself about it. Suddenly realizing that you haven't stopped to see how you feel for weeks could be a sign that you're afraid to look at what you know.

We're all familiar with the feeling of knowing something intuitively and talking ourselves out of acting on it. Maybe you notice he drinks quite a bit every time you see him, but you justify it by saying he just likes to have a good time instead of admitting what you know to be true: He has a drinking problem. Or you notice that a coworker gives you the heebie-jeebies and you think it must just be you—until you find out that three other women in the office feel the same way around him. When you find yourself rationalizing his behavior somehow, your intuition is trying to tell you something.

## Watch for Red Flags Waving in the Wind

You certainly can run into trouble by not tuning in to your intuition or ignoring what it tells you.

Part of the purpose of dating is to gather clues and use them to make a judgment about your potential partner. Keep your eyes open and you don't have to worry that you'll marry someone who has a serious problem that you didn't see. For example, if he doesn't call when he says he will, that's a red flag. So is catching him in a lie. If these types of incidents occur early in a relationship, there's no reason to give him another chance to let you down or deceive you. Better to forget about him altogether.

Naturally, he's not going to wear a sign that advertises any of his defects, but he will tell you about himself in ways that are almost as obvious. Your job is to pay attention when he sends up a red flag. Below are some examples of things that are symptomatic of addiction or alcoholism.

- He uses illegal drugs.
- He uses prescription drugs to get high.
- His personality changes when he drinks.
- He wishes other people would just mind their own business about how much he drinks.
- He misses work because of drinking.
- He's been cited for driving under the influence.
- He drinks almost every time you see him.
- He drinks every day.

These are signs that he may have a violent streak:

- His ex-girlfriend accused him of hitting her.
- He states that when a man hits a woman it makes you wonder what she did to provoke him.

- He has severe mood swings.
- There is a history of physical abuse in his family.
- He is cruel to animals.
- He destroys property in anger.
- He pressures you for sex.

These symptoms reflect a probable philanderer:

- He cheated on a former girlfriend or wife.
- His father or other male role model was unfaithful in his relationships.
- He says men aren't built to be faithful to one woman for their entire life.
- He hits on other women while he's with you.
- He has an extensive collection of pornographic movies or magazines, or he subscribes to pornographic Web sites.
- He sometimes offers explanations that don't add up about why he was late, where he was last night, what he does for a living, etc.
- He refuses to use a condom or to demonstrate that he's free of diseases with a doctor's report.
- He's dating you while he's still married—even if he's separated or divorcing.

## Sharpening Your Intuition

*Intuition is a spiritual faculty and does not explain, but simply points the way.*

—Florence Scovel Shinn

Think of the times you've known something was coming even though you had no way of knowing it was. Your subconscious had put together clues that you weren't even tuned in to consciously to give you a premonition of sorts. That's what our subconscious does. That makes it an invaluable tool in dating, when we're putting our hearts at risk and would very often like to know the future. You can't know the future, but you can certainly make a reasonable prediction.

For instance, Wanda couldn't put her finger on why Todd made her uncomfortable. He was well dressed and gentlemanly when she met him at a work-related convention. When he asked her if he could call her, she couldn't think of any logical reason to refuse him, so she gave him her cell phone number. Afterward, she had time to reflect on how she felt when he was pursuing her and concluded that she wouldn't go out with him. Although she didn't know why, she knew she didn't feel comfortable with him.

Todd never did call Wanda, but two weeks later a woman who described herself as Todd's wife called to find out if she had been sleeping with her husband.

Did Wanda know that Todd was married when he was flirting with her? Not exactly. Did she know that something was amiss? Absolutely. How she knew was not important, but following her instinct was.

As long as you're taking time to listen to and follow your intuition and you know what problems to take seriously, you will *not* unknowingly pick a man with a serious defect or who simply isn't right for you. Even if you've made terrible choices with men in the past, you won't do it again if you commit to honor your intuition and to use the information in this book about which kinds of men to avoid.

If you follow your instincts, you can avoid the heartbreak of investing in a man who will definitely let you down. You can also stop worrying about whether you're headed down the road to disaster and just enjoy the mating dance.

To keep your instincts sharp, avoid using alcohol on your first few dates with a guy. I know it's tempting to drink to loosen up a bit or be social, but drinking impairs your judgment. If you're trying to learn about the man you're with, you're better off to keep all your wits about you.

Altered states of any kind—and that includes sex—will impair your judgment. Therefore, you'll want to give yourself time to make up your mind about him before you engage with him sexually. Unfortunately, Anita had a much harder time tuning in to her heart about Patrick because she had sex with him on their first date. She felt euphoric around him, which compromised her objectivity.

Soon Anita learned things about Patrick she couldn't ignore. He complained that some "real bitches" at his work were telling other women to avoid him because he was only interested in sex. He made derogatory comments about women in general, and when Anita objected to this, he hung up on her. That's when Anita realized that Patrick was probably a womanizer who had jilted women at his workplace. She felt foolish for letting him take advantage of her too.

"I didn't see him clearly because I was already so bonded to him," she confessed. "But he was so awful, I had to acknowledge that I made a mistake."

So much for Patrick.

## When You Have a Hunch It's Gonna Be Good, You're Probably Right

> *To love another person is to see the face of God.*
>
> —Victor Hugo

Listening to and following an instinct that things are right is just as powerful as paying attention to a feeling that something is wrong. For instance, you might have the sense after just one date that you will be spending the rest of your life with a certain guy. If that's what your intuition is telling you, it may be true! Women often tell me they realized when they first met their husbands that this was the man they would marry. It happens all the time. If you're going to trust your intuition to tell you when something's wrong, it's also fair to trust it when it's telling you that something is very right.

My sister-in-law knew the minute she met her husband that she was going to marry him. My agent had a strong hunch when he first met his wife that he would marry her. So don't be surprised if you find yourself "knowing" something you can't possibly know—like who you'll be growing old with.

## Slurping Cereal Is Not a Capital Offense

What if the good guy you're dating is always late, doesn't make much money, or lets the dishes pile up in the sink? You may find these practices irritating, but none of them indicates a time bomb that will destroy your relationship in the future. Everything else is just small stuff, which, as you know, you don't have to sweat. As long as you marry a good guy, everything else is workable, and chances are very good that you can stay happily married for the rest of your life.

Once you've gone out with a man enough to know that he is not one of the jerks who uses, cheats, or physically hurts women, you can relax into the relationship without worrying that you are taking an unnecessary risk. You can be confident that you're dating a good guy—not a perfect man, but one with whom you can have a wonderful relationship. You're not eliminating *all* risk, since you could certainly be disappointed if the romance ended, but you are eliminating surefire heartbreak. Now the odds of developing a passionate, healthy, long-term relationship are greatly in your favor.

# 19

# YOU'LL RECOGNIZE THE MAN WHO'S RIGHT FOR YOU

*Anyone can be passionate, but it takes real lovers to be silly.*

—Rose Franken

***Feelings of attraction for a reliable man are often less intense than the feelings of euphoria you experience around a man who is unreliable.***

***The key is to look for the more subtle feelings of attraction, which often sneak up on you, instead of dismissing someone because you don't feel constantly euphoric around him.***

***You will soon find yourself falling for a man who's as dependable as the sunrise.***

## How to Recognize *Your* Good Guy

A man who does not fall into one of the three bad-guy categories (addicted, abusive, or chronically unfaithful) is a good guy—not a perfect man, but one who is capable of being loyal, faithful, and adoring.

Of course, that doesn't necessarily mean he is the guy for you. Not just *any* good guy will do.

So how will you be able to pick your good guy out of the crowd? There are just two more things you need to be sure of:

- that you're attracted to him, and
- that he treats you well.

When you meet someone who fits those criteria, he could very well be your guy.

## The Essence of Attraction

> *In a great romance, each person plays a part*
> *the other really likes.*
>
> —Elizabeth Ashley

Sometimes it's easy to tell if you're attracted to someone. You're weak in the knees, nervous when you're with him, and exceptionally happy that he's pursuing you. That is all part of the thrill of being with the man who's right for you.

Yet being attracted to someone doesn't mean that you will consistently feel they are completely wonderful every second. In fact, being a woman pretty much guarantees that you will have moments when you're downright repelled by something about a man to whom you are generally attracted. Don't let the ups and downs throw you. The trick is to look at the big picture. Ask yourself: Do I feel good when I'm with him? Do I enjoy his touch? Does he make me happy? Do I miss him when I don't see him for a few days? Do I think he's smart and handsome? Does he make me laugh?

If so, then you're attracted to him, and the future of the relationship is bright.

## Beware the Unreliable Man

Dating a good guy you're not doing back flips about might be a good move for you if you have a history of falling for unpredictable men. We all want a man who will show up and call when he says he will. Unfortunately, unreliable men can seem very exciting because of the lure of random reinforcement.

A laboratory rat will push a lever to get food only when he's hungry so long as the food comes out every time he pushes it. If pushing the lever produces food only occasionally, then the rat feels compelled to push the lever incessantly. This is not so different from the thrill of pulling the handle on a slot machine and hoping to win the jackpot. The powerful draw of random reinforcement creates a sense of excitement and unpredictability that makes people feel euphoric when they finally get a payoff.

The same thing happens in dating. When someone you're attracted to says he'll call or show up but sometimes doesn't, it's both frustrating and exhilarating to date him. His unpredictability adds an element of excitement that you come to associate with him personally. You might begin to confuse falling in love with the incredible I-just-won-the-jackpot high you feel when Mr. Inconsistent actually does what he says he is going to do.

That's why a man who is less than reliable can seem more exciting than a Steady Eddy. In fact, if you're dating two guys at once, the one who is as dependable as the sunrise might even seem boring compared to the unreliable one. You don't get that same adrenaline rush when you see the guy you know will be there.

Even worse, since you'll never get that intense feeling from a man you can count on, you might begin to think you're not attracted to good guys. What you're really saying is that you don't feel the same level of *intensity* with someone you can count on. That doesn't mean you won't feel excitement and affection for a guy you can trust.

Patty began to associate feelings of anxiety and high adrenaline with Chuck. After the high drama of that relationship—wondering if he would show up for their dates, feeling extremely disappointed when he didn't, and ecstatic if he did—dating someone reliable seemed dull. But falling in love isn't dull. It's subtler than what Patty felt around Chuck, but it's not dull.

## IF HE DOESN'T EXCITE YOU, HE'S NOT THE RIGHT GUY FOR YOU

*Love is friendship set on fire.*

—JEREMY TAYLOR

If you're accustomed to dating cheaters, users, or abusers, a good guy won't give you the same feeling of intensity that you're used to. However, that doesn't mean you're not attracted to him. Take it slow and hang in as long as you can to give yourself a chance to feel affection and delight without anxiety. If after at least three dates you still don't want to kiss him, don't try to force it. You're not attracted to him, so move along.

Remember the story about Amy—the woman who wasn't initially attracted to Carl but ended up completely falling for him as she got to know him? Carl's warmth and masculinity more than compensated for what she at first thought were his ordinary looks. But sometimes just the opposite happens. Sometimes you will feel initial physical attraction that diminishes as you get to know your date. That's because even the best-looking man in the world won't hold your interest if there's no chemistry between you.

This was Kendra's situation when she met Peter. She thought he was good-looking. She knew through friends that he was truly a good guy, gentlemanly, sweet, and loyal. Sure enough, he treated her like a princess and made it clear that he adored her.

But something was wrong. Right after their first date, her attraction to Peter seemed to diminish. She continued to see him, but over time noticed that she was avoiding touching him or kissing him. Three months later, she had to admit that she simply wasn't attracted to him and never would be. She wondered if she was sabotaging a relationship with great potential.

If Kendra had had a history of choosing bad guys, I would attribute her disinterest in Peter to his not providing the adrenaline high of random reinforcement. But Kendra didn't have that history. She had given herself ample time to develop affection with Peter. That meant that there really was something missing in the chemistry for her. Difficult though it was, she had to end her relationship with Peter.

Although she was disappointed that she couldn't make this great guy into the right guy for her, she was relieved to stop trying to force attraction that wasn't there.

But what about their initial meeting? She was drawn to him initially—before she knew anything about him yet—but that attraction was mostly physical. The more she got to know him, the less his good looks could compensate for a personality that didn't match hers.

## Don't Rush to Judgment

> *We seek the comfort of another. Someone to share the life we choose. Someone to help us through the never-ending attempt to understand ourselves. And in the end, someone to comfort us along the way.*
>
> —Marlin Finch Lupus

Feelings of attraction can fluctuate, so it's best not to rush to judgment about them. For instance, Stella was crazy about Tim until he seemed cranky on their third date. Luckily, on their fourth date, he apologized that he had been in such bad spirits the last time he'd seen her. As he apologized, she realized that she too had been a little snippy the night of their third date, so she also expressed regret for her behavior. Not only was she attracted to him again, she was impressed with his maturity. They learned early on that they could work through everyday problems and come out on the other side.

Fortunately, Stella remembered how she felt on the first two dates in deciding to try going out with Tim again, rather than focusing on the third date, which turned out to be an aberration. The wisdom of taking this approach is that you're less likely to end a promising relationship because one of you is having an off night.

## Signs He's Treating You Well

Attraction is the first half of the litmus test in finding your good guy. The second half is to be sure your potential beau treats you well. Just for the record, a man who is treating you well will:

- make plans to see you;
- give you compliments, presents, and an enjoyable evening (which doesn't mean that he has to spend wads of cash on you—just that he wants to share what he's got);
- try to please you by making you laugh, remembering your favorite dessert, or checking to see if you're comfortable.

You are *not* being treated well if he:

- doesn't make an effort to see you, only makes an effort to see you to have sex, or stands you up;

- expects you to pay for yourself whenever the two of you go out;
- pays more attention to other women than he does to you.

Making time to see you and call you are components of good treatment from a man, but it's important to note that in the very early stages of dating, he might take a week or two to call and make a second date. That doesn't mean he's not treating you well—just that it's still early. After you're in an exclusive relationship, a man who is treating you well would make time to see you at least a couple of times a week.

If you're attracted to a good guy who treats you well, you can go full-speed ahead into this relationship without worrying that you're making a bad choice. However imperfect he is in other ways matters little. What difference does it make if he yells at the TV during a sporting event as long as he goes out of his way to make sure you're comfortable when you're together? Who cares if he chews with his mouth open sometimes when he sends you your favorite flowers because you had a bad day? You can fall for a guy who thinks demolition derbies are the highest form of entertainment as long as you melt when you see him. He has the ability to make you happy, if you let him, so why would you turn him away?

## You Have the Power to Accept or Reject

> *When we criticize another person, it says nothing about that person; it merely says something about our own need to be critical.*
>
> —Richard Carlson

As much as you might like to, you simply can't change a man who doesn't treat you well. A Surrendered Single gives up the illusion that her date is her fixer-upper project.

Surrendering means you give up trying to control someone else and focus that energy on yourself. It also means you come into acceptance and even gratitude that everything is just as it should be.

Therefore, even if he's gorgeous and has a promising career, you don't want to invest any more time in a man who doesn't spend his time and energy adoring, thrilling, and pleasing you just for the pleasure of seeing you happy.

If you find that a man you're seeing doesn't treat you well, then it's important to break off that dating relationship immediately for the same reason you'd stop seeing a man who wasn't a good guy: You deserve a passionate union with a safe man.

Unfortunately, it's not easy to let go of someone who has a lot of the things you want in a man, even if he isn't doting on you. You might think, *Maybe he'll start making time to see me when his work slows a little, or when his kids go back to their mother's, or after the football season ends.* But that kind of thinking will keep you hanging on to something that just isn't good enough for you. With a guy like that, you'll really be tempted to try to control him by cajoling, begging, or bribing him, because you'll never feel like you're getting enough attention.

If you're lonely and have been for a while, it's easy to rationalize that he's better than nothing or that he doesn't treat you *that* badly. Once you head down that path, though, you're setting yourself up for disappointment. If the basics aren't there, nothing else matters. And until you let go of a man who doesn't treat you well or to whom you aren't attracted, you won't have the space in your life to welcome the man who's right for you.

# 20

# DON'T USE SEX TO CONTROL THE RELATIONSHIP

*Sex is hardly ever just about sex.*
—Shirley MacLaine

*Practice good self-care and protect yourself by making sure that you're physically and emotionally safe before you have sex with a man you're dating.*

*To minimize the risk of heartbreak, get to know him for at least one month* and *go out with him on at least six dates (whichever takes longer) before you engage with him sexually. Make sure that your relationship is exclusive. Tell him about the things that you think make you unlovable to make sure that the man you're with is capable of loving you just as you are, rather than how you would like to appear.*

## You Can Control When You First Have Sex

Surrendering isn't about following rules. It's about gracefully accepting the things that are beyond your control and focusing on what is within your power.

Deciding when you will first have sex with the man you're dating is entirely in your command. A Surrendered Single takes care of herself by making sure that she is physically and emotionally safe before agreeing to commence a physical relationship. The longer you take to know him, the more you can ensure your emotional and physical safety.

Since it takes at least a month to determine if a man is a good guy, a Surrendered Single won't expose herself to unnecessary risk by undressing with him before she's known him *at least* that long and dated him *at least* six times. I say *at least* because some women will hear their hearts telling them to wait longer than that. Some women will want to wait for marriage to be that intimate. The point is to honor yourself by waiting until it's right for you.

A Surrendered Single wouldn't risk her health or her emotional well-being by becoming one of multiple sex partners, so she insists on an exclusive agreement with her beau before she engages sexually in any way, including oral sex, manual stimulation, or intercourse.

## Free Love Costs Too Much

Once upon a time I assumed that if I were sexual with a guy I just met, that would automatically make me his girlfriend. Now it sounds so naïve that it's embarrassing to admit that I thought experiencing the vulnerability of physical intimacy would bind us emotionally. Naturally, my sex-as-a-route-to-a-committed-relationship method never worked.

It was my way of trying to control the trajectory of the relationship. Sex was my unspoken but very forceful attempt to make him seal the deal.

Often, when a one-night stand is over, the woman may be thinking, *He really likes me!* while the man feels no desire to pursue anything more than a sexual relationship. The potential for disaster is high.

The good news is that if you actually date a guy for a while by sharing movies, conversation, and meals, you become more than just a sex object. In fact, your chances of bonding with him romantically improve dramatically because he's not triggered into the coyote-caught-in-a-trap mode that often follows first- or second-date sex. If you go on several dates before you have sex with a man, there is a good chance that a romance might develop. If, on the other hand, you have sex with a man right upon meeting him, you have given the nonsexual but very intimate part of the relationship little chance of developing. You'll feel vulnerable after you have sex with him, and you can't control how he reacts afterward. A Surrendered Single sets limits to improve her safety beforehand.

## Let Dating Casually Lead to Dating Exclusively

Part of your birthright as a woman is having a man woo you to win your love and the right to be his exclusively. If he's pursued you since the very first date, chances are he will continue. Just as he took the initiative to ask you out in the first place, he'll also take the initiative to tell you when he:

- no longer wants to see anyone else;
- has fallen in love with you;
- wants to make love to you;
- wants to marry you.

Therefore, you don't need to control these relationship benchmarks by bringing up these topics. You especially never need to say "We need to talk" as a prelude to getting him to say that he loves you or wants to date you exclusively. Instead, allow the transition from casual dating to becoming boyfriend and girlfriend happen naturally. If you surrender control, you will undoubtedly enjoy the pleasure of having him pursue you for an exclusive relationship. That, in turn, will raise your confidence in him and in the relationship. You won't be plagued by wondering if he is as invested as you are.

Luckily for me, I was so unsophisticated when I met John I didn't even think about whether we should be exclusive and when it would happen. I just enjoyed myself when I was with him. Then one day after a movie he said, "I don't want to see anyone else but you." I admitted that I didn't want to see anyone else either. Just as he had asked me out to begin with, he had taken us to the next step without any prompting from me.

Looking back, I think my complete lack of anxiety about the status of our relationship—combined with my consistent enthusiasm for him—made it easier for him to broach the topic of exclusivity.

If you don't manipulate, cajole, control, insist, or demand that a man ask you to be his, chances are good he will think of it himself and bring it up when he's ready.

As always, continue to smile at everyone and accept dates with other men, even if you're really interested only in him.

Since you're still flirting with and dating other people, you don't have to worry about when one will ask to see you exclusively. You have other options. Of course, that's hard to remember when you've got your hopes up about one in particular. However, trying to get him to commit will actually hinder him from doing just that, since he then has to overcome his reluctance to be manipulated.

## Set Your Limits Around Sex

*Put your ear down close to your soul and listen hard.*

—Anne Sexton

But what if he doesn't bring it up? What if you go out with a guy you're crazy about week after week and he never says anything about not seeing anyone else?

Let it go—until he tries to have sex with you.

When his desire to have sex with you comes up before he's brought up the topic of dating exclusively, you will have to tell him your policy: You won't have sex outside of an exclusive relationship. This is different from insisting he commit to you. Rather, you're simply stating your own limitations and letting him choose what to do next. It may be tempting to say something like, "You have to show me you're serious first," but that would be an attempt to control him. The Surrendered approach is to speak only for yourself: "I have to know I'm in an exclusive relationship first."

As you can imagine, telling him this probably will motivate him to start talking about going steady on the spot. He may say something like, "I don't want to see anyone but you. And I'm not just saying that so we can have sex."

If *you* want to date only him, then the question is, should you believe him? Once he says he's seeing you and you alone, should you have sex with him on the spot?

Some creeps will say they want to be exclusive with you—even if they don't mean it—just to have sex. But a good guy won't do that. A good guy who doesn't want to be your boyfriend for whatever reason will respect your conditions and back off if he can't meet them. Since you will have dated the man in question for at least a month before you consider getting physically intimate with him, you'll have a very good idea about whether he's a good guy. In that time, your intuition will have been at work.

If you're still evaluating him to see if he's a good man, it's definitely not a good idea to sleep with him before you've decided. Take it as slow as you need to.

## Sex Impairs Your Judgment

*Some things are better than sex, and some things are worse, but there's nothing exactly like it.*

—W. C. Fields

One of the reasons to delay having sex with a man you're seeing, no matter how much heat the two of you are generating, is that like alcohol, sex impairs your judgment.

Since the power of surrendering is in the ability to accept or reject the man you're dating, you don't want to do anything that will impair your ability to reject a man who's not right for you. Premature sex can hamper your judgment. In addition to creating a feeling of having a glorious connection to your date, having sex is a mind-altering experience. Once you feel the physical closeness and vulnerability of sex, you'll have a harder time seeing him objectively, which means you're more likely to dismiss red flags.

That's why having sex with a man before he's proven himself to be a good guy who treats you well puts you in the high-risk category for heartbreak.

## Sex Won't Make Him Stay

*No man can be held throughout the day by what happens throughout the night.*

—Sally Stanford

Physical attraction and passion are powerfully tempting forces, and waiting a month before having sex can sometimes seem like an eternity.

Even more overpowering is the feeling that if we don't have sex with him soon he might lose interest and then we'll be alone. Again.

If you're anything like I was, you may be using sex to control a man to be right where you want him—with you. The problem with using this kind of control to maintain a relationship is that it doesn't work and we cheat ourselves of being genuinely desired and pursued. If you use sex to keep him around, then you'll never know if he likes you just for you.

## Make Safety a Prerequisite

Even if you think he's a good man who's telling the truth, there's one more thing you'll want to have before you engage sexually with anyone: proof that he's not going to give you a potentially deadly sexually transmitted disease.

As part of your self-care, you'll want to suggest that you get HIV tests together. Since that takes some time (and further investment into the relationship on his part), you'll find out if he's telling the truth when you make this test a prerequisite to physical intimacy. You can raise this topic in a nonthreatening way by saying, "Let's go get HIV tests done together, so we both feel safe."

I know this can be an awkward and uncomfortable conversation, but it serves as another brick in the foundation of a relationship that's built on intimacy, health, and consideration. His willingness to honor your wishes is further evidence that he's invested in your relationship. Conversely, his reluctance to agree to this reasonable request to ensure your safety—and his own!—will speak volumes about his lack of commitment.

## Give Up Control of Your Image

*At last I know what love is really like.*

—Virgil

Everyone has done things they're embarrassed about or ashamed of. Maybe you'd rather he didn't know you joined AA or had an abortion. Perhaps you're ashamed that you've been divorced twice or flunked out of college. Whatever you're embarrassed about will eventually come out in the course of a committed relationship anyway, so you might as well tell him those things *before* you become physically intimate.

The logic behind this suggestion is that if he accepts you the way you are after hearing the things you're least proud of, you don't have to worry that he'll leave you later when he learns more about you. If you reveal yourself and he doesn't approve for whatever reason, you'll be glad that you learned that before you bonded with him sexually. If you wait until after you've made yourself vulnerable by having sex, and he decides not to stick around, you're going to feel lousy. Granted, you'll feel lousy if he breaks up with you anyway, but if you've already had sex, you'll feel worse.

Another benefit of disclosing your secrets is that showing all your cards will cultivate a stronger emotional connection. You'll feel wonderful knowing that even though he knows all about you, he still wants to be with you and only you.

Remember that in order to have an intimate relationship, you must be vulnerable. If you're physically intimate before you reveal your innermost secrets, you're keeping your defenses up in a way that doesn't serve you. I don't recommend making the first date a confessional. But at some point before you climb into bed together, make sure that you're convinced that he likes you for you—warts and all.

## Don't Become Part of a Harem

A Surrendered Single is willing to venture her heart when necessary to find the romance and companionship she craves, but she's not foolhardy. She recognizes the different risk factors associated with each stage of a romantic relationship and behaves accordingly. For instance, to go out on a date with someone one time she has only to venture her evening, which is a relatively small risk.

Having sex with a man, however, is a big risk for a Surrendered Single. No matter how she tells herself she will stay detached and treat it as a casual event, a woman who wants to be in a committed relationship will never find this satisfying. Therefore, she does whatever she can to make sure she is safe before she makes this big investment, including making sure the relationship is exclusive.

Without that piece, the risk is just too great. Sure, it might all work out in the end, but why take chances when you don't have to?

# 21

# THERE'S NOTHING TO FEAR BUT YOUR URGE TO CONTROL HIM

*To fear love is to fear life.*
—BERTRAND RUSSELL

*There's always some risk in committing to someone else, because you can't control whether he'll keep his end of the bargain. If you find yourself wanting reassurance from your boyfriend, try to bite your tongue. Keep your eyes and heart open to his efforts, however subtle, to make you happy. Trust that he wants to make you happy and will look for ways to please you.*

*When you're unhappy about something in your relationship, you may be tempted to instruct, criticize, or correct your boyfriend. Instead, turn inward and ask yourself what it is you're feeling and what you want. That's the important information you'll need to express yourself in a way that is effective, nonthreatening, and dignified. For best results, start your sentences with "I feel . . ." and "I want . . ." when you address the problem. The trick is to control yourself and to give him the opportunity to meet your desires without trying to control him.*

*When you relinquish control, you won't have to worry about the relationship ending or a future divorce. Nothing improves the odds of having a lasting marriage like nurturing intimacy and passion.*

*Making these changes will be very challenging at times, but you don't have to do this alone. Find a happily married woman to mentor you and rely on her support to help you form new habits.*

## Don't Ask No-Win Questions

Perhaps the most tempting reason to try to control your boyfriend is to get reassurance.

- Does he like me?
- Does this relationship have a future?
- Does he think I'm beautiful?
- Is he the type who will commit to me?

We all feel vulnerable in a new relationship because we don't know where we stand. Asking him any of these questions, however, is an unfair setup. Even if you get the answer you want, it will sound hollow because you forced it. Worse still, asking such questions puts an unnecessary strain on a relationship that's just getting started. Weighing it down with those big expectations for the future is like urging a child to become a doctor when she enters kindergarten. Putting that much pressure on anyone is smothering.

What you really want is for him to want to tell you he likes you, loves you, finds you beautiful, and wants to be with you for life. To get that, you'll have to wait until he feels the time is right to say it, and you can't control when that time is going to be. Your only option is to surrender.

If you find yourself feeling insecure, see if you can find comfort in his actions instead of longing for the words. When he hugs and kisses you, holds your hand, takes you out, listens to your problems, helps you assemble your patio furniture, pumps gas for you, or gives you his jacket, he is showing his affection and attraction in ways that are more significant than words.

If you take inventory of his actions and realize that not only is he not saying he wants to be with you, there isn't much evidence from his deeds either, that's a different story. The source of your insecurity in that case is realizing on some level that he's probably never going to say those words to you, in which case he's not the right man for you.

Either way, you can't make him tell you he likes you. Even if you could, extracting such a confession would never be satisfying. You *can* go on with your life by focusing on your self-care instead of on what he is or isn't saying. The less urgent you feel about getting his reassurance, the more attractive you'll be, and the more likely you are to get them.

## Get a Second Opinion

> *What is it about friendship that makes being among friends so much richer than being among the most accomplished and interesting strangers?*
>
> —Sandy Sheehy

Instead of asking him manipulative questions, talk to a friend—preferably a happily married woman—for perspective when you're feeling vulnerable. Ask her to reflect back to you the evidence that a man is interested in you. Tell your friend your hopes and fears and let her encourage or comfort you as necessary.

While you might still feel some free-floating terror when you're with him, at least you'll have the comfort of a reality check from someone who listens well and tells you what she sees. The temptation to force his hand will lessen.

In turn, your ability to go with the flow will give your budding relationship the best opportunity to thrive. Choose intimacy instead of control and your relationship will very likely become the passionate union you've always dreamed of having.

## What I Had to Learn to Stay Married

As a single woman, you are in the habit of running everything in your life, and rightly so. Now that you're becoming part of a twosome, you may feel the temptation to try to run his life, too—at least some of the time. Ironically, one of the keys to keeping your relationship strong will be to continue to do just as you did before you met him: focus on yourself.

I know it's difficult to refrain from making helpful suggestions when somebody else's actions are impacting you by making you late, leaving you more to clean, or causing you to throw out the spoiled cold cuts that were out on the counter all night. Of course, you would always want to express your feelings in any of those situations, but what you don't want to do is correct, criticize, belittle, or dismiss him in an effort to make him more efficient. You may know a quicker way to hang a picture, but unless you want to be hanging the picture alone, it's important to honor the way he does things. Having your own way is satisfying, but having someone to cuddle and laugh with is even better.

Unfortunately, I hadn't learned that when I married John. As a result, I frequently bickered with him about how to make the bed instead of just appreciating that he'd made it. That narrow, shortsighted focus almost cost me my marriage.

When I surrendered by acknowledging that the only person I can ever change is myself, I discovered that my husband really wants to make me happy and that his loyalty to me is greater than I imagined. Now—just as when we first met—he takes great pride in protecting, cherishing, and helping me. He's willing to grow and move forward as I grow and move forward, and I often feel that I get more than I give.

If your romance is just starting out, you probably don't have to stretch to realize that he wants you to be happy, and that he's worthy of your respect. You have the right perspective: The things that make the two of you different are also wonderful. This part of surrendering is easy at this stage because it feels natural. As it becomes a habit, surrendering will go a long way toward keeping the passion and romance high long after your boyfriend becomes your husband. He will continue to want to please you for years to come.

It's not just my husband who responds with tenderness and generosity when I treat him with respect and relinquish control of his life. Good men the world over respond to their wives the same way. Now that I've watched many thousands of women successfully use surrendering in their marriages, I've come to realize that wives have tremendous power to make or break a happy union.

## The Difference Between Work and Love

> *Nothing takes the taste out of peanut butter quite like unrequited love.*
>
> —Charlie Brown

Depending on where you work, it may be second nature for you to take charge, call out orders, and correct others as part of doing your job. But since the goals of work (efficiency, a promotion, profit) are very different from the goals of dating (togetherness, connection, affection), it follows that you'll need a different approach in the dating arena.

For instance, my husband once dated a third-grade teacher who had trouble changing gears when she left work to meet with him. She would say "Go sit down" and "put that away" as if he were an eight-year-old student. As you can imagine, this wasn't conducive to the kind of romantic partnership either of them wanted.

Bridget recalled a first-date brunch where she immediately started to order the wait staff around before he had a chance to say anything. "He had brought me there," she said, "and here I was calling all the shots like I was in charge. Next time, I think I'll wait a while before I demonstrate how competent I am at a restaurant," she joked.

Competence is, of course, an attractive quality, but your boyfriend does not want to play the part of underling while you orchestrate everything single-handedly. You'll never get to be his partner by acting like the boss. You will only emasculate him.

Part of connecting with someone else is admitting that you don't want to do everything yourself, don't have all the answers, and sometimes need help. I'm not suggesting that you dumb down or pretend to be incapable, just that you take time off from running the show when you're with your man.

## He Can't Read Your Mind

*If we knew each other's secrets,*
*what comforts we should find.*
—John Churton Collins

Joanne was trying hard not to control her boyfriend but found herself getting upset because he spent an hour and a half looking around a sporting goods store. "I agreed to go with him, but I expect him to be more considerate of my time," she complained. Joanne didn't tell her boyfriend that she wanted to leave the store, so he had no way of knowing, since she was also browsing to amuse herself. "I shouldn't *have* to tell him, because that's just common courtesy," she insisted.

But what Joanne was really saying is that she expected him to read her mind, and nobody can do that. She felt awkward—maybe even a little rude—saying what she wanted, but there's nothing inconsiderate about simply stating your preference, as in "I'd like to get going." In fact, expressing your desires is a critical part of having an intimate relationship.

Some of us were taught not to say what we want. We were told that we shouldn't be so selfish, that we shouldn't crave so much. But knowing what you want and expressing it plainly are attractive qualities. It shows that we hold ourselves in high regard and know our own hearts and minds. That's certainly preferable to not saying what we want and then growing resentful because we don't have the things that would make us happy.

Joanne was afraid that saying what she wanted was the same as trying to control her man. "Isn't he just going to feel like he has to do what I say I want?" she wondered. But expressing your desires isn't the same as exerting control, because it doesn't require anything of anyone else. You're just speaking for yourself. Trying to get what you want by making demands, complaints, or having expectations, on the other hand, is about trying to control him. For instance, Joanne could have said:

> ***Demand:*** "You better get me out of here before I get cranky."
> ***Complaint:*** "I can't stand to be in this stupid store for one more minute."
> ***Expectation:*** "I want you to get me out of this store right now."
> ***Desire:*** "I want to go soon" or "I don't want to stay here much longer."

Naturally, Joanne had the best chance of getting what she wanted and preserving the intimacy by simply expressing her desire without making a demand, as in the last example. Learning to express your desires is always a good habit to develop. Learning to say what you want in a romantic relationship is especially critical, because your partner needs that information so he can make you happy.

## He Wants You to Have What You Want

> *A good marriage is like a good trade:*
> *Each thinks he got the better deal.*
> —Ivern Ball

But what if Joanne's boyfriend wanted to stay at the sporting goods store?

That happens sometimes, but since your happiness is a high priority to the good guy that you're dating, he will weigh your desires heavily in his decision making. I know this because I've asked thousands of men how important it is to them that the woman they're involved with is happy, and they all agree: "It's *very* important"; "It's imperative"; "It's paramount"; "It's everything."

"It's the most important thing."

That's not to say that your every desire will be met, but it does mean that your guy will go out of his way to give you what he can.

For instance, if Joanne's boyfriend had known that he could make her happy by leaving the store, perhaps he would have taken the opportunity to please her by going right then. Since he didn't know, he had no such opportunity to meet her desire. Perhaps he wouldn't have been able to leave the store right then, but he might have come up with another solution. Maybe he would have offered her the keys to turn on the radio and the air conditioning in the car while he hurried to complete his business, or agreed to meet her in a nearby clothing store when he was finished.

The point is to recognize that he will take your feelings into account, but only if he knows what they are.

Helen was having trouble believing that a man really would be that concerned with her happiness when she started seeing Todd. One night after he'd taken her out to dinner, she mentioned that she wanted to return something at a clothing store, which was closing in half an hour. She didn't say, "I want you to take me" or "I want to return it tonight," but Todd immediately asked for the check, paid it in a hurry, and drove her to the store as quickly as he could. She felt awkward having him there in the clothing store with her, and it was clear that he wouldn't have gone there normally—except to make her happy. "I kept saying to myself, 'receive, receive, receive.' I couldn't believe he would do that for me, because no guy ever has before," she said. "But I better get used to it, because it looks like he's not going anywhere."

## How "Harmless" Comments Can Hurt

> *There is a courtesy of the heart; it is allied to love. From it springs the purest courtesy in the outward behavior.*
>
> —Johann Wolfgang von Goethe

If you find yourself telling your boyfriend to take a nap before he eats, diversify his portfolio, or rinse the dishes before he puts them in the dishwasher, you've gone from being the girlfriend to being the boss. If you remind him it's time to go to the dentist, show him how to iron his shirt, or warn him to eat less cholesterol, you're now trying to run his life.

While to you these comments may seem harmless or even helpful, they're actually covert criticisms:

***Actual comment:*** "Why don't you take a nap and then eat?"
***Implied criticism:*** I know better than you what your body needs.
***Actual comment:*** "You should rinse the dishes before you put them in the dishwasher."
***Implied criticism:*** You don't do the dishes the right way.
***Actual comment:*** "You're supposed to diversify your investments."
***Implied criticism:*** You're not a wise investor.

Since running two adult lives is too much for any one person, attempting it puts you squarely on the road to romantic disaster. Either you'll feel resentful that you do everything and lose respect for him, or he'll get tired of feeling like he's with his mother and dump you—or both. Either way, you diminish him and overburden yourself. Worst of all, you've squashed any possibility for intimacy. No one wants to crawl into bed with his mother or his boss.

A therapist described a client who was seriously considering whether to marry her boyfriend even though she described him as an incompetent blockhead. The therapist pointed out that the woman showed very little respect for her boyfriend and said that she didn't see how the couple could go on together when they were both so unhappy. The woman's boyfriend was her opposite in many ways, and she thought that she wanted someone like herself. When she considered ending the relationship, however, she suddenly became aware of the qualities she admired in him, like his warm humor, his sense of adventure, and his complete loyalty to her.

Faced with losing him, she realized that they complemented each other.

Even so, this woman couldn't resist telling her boyfriend that he was driving too fast, putting too much milk on his cereal, and wasting his money buying occasional lottery tickets. Feeling he couldn't do anything right, he stopped trying to do anything at all. Irritated and defensive, the boyfriend began to withdraw until he was barely in the relationship.

Instead of fanning the flames of romance by respecting his decisions, she fell into the pattern of telling him what to do, which set an unpleasant precedent. While she may have thought she was helping him become the kind of man she wanted to be with, she was really extinguishing the embers of intimacy. She was also preventing the relationship from ever advancing to its highest level and possibly from moving forward at all.

If you identify with the woman in this story, it may be that the root of your comments is genuine concern for him. More likely, though, you are thinking of your own needs, which is fine *as long as you speak for yourself about yourself.*

For instance, maybe you want him to nap first and then eat instead of the other way around because you want to be able to eat together later when you're hungry. In that circumstance, it seems perfectly logical to suggest that he wait to eat until later. Instead of telling him what to do, however, you'll have more success and intimacy if you focus on yourself. Tell him what you want and how you feel by saying, "I'm not hungry right now, but I would like to eat with you later." Then, instead of following your orders, he can decide if he wants to snack, wait to eat with you, or take a rain check.

Reminding him to rinse the dishes might seem like an effective way to avoid having to chisel off the stuck-on food, but the accompanying insult will cost you dearly in terms of lost intimacy. That's because the subtext of your comment is "You won't do it right unless I tell you how," which is neither endearing nor kind. If you decide you simply must try to control him, you are actually deciding to forsake intimacy.

Instead, consider saying how you feel, as in "I hate having to pry things off the dishes." You can't make him change his habits, but since he wants to please you, he may work to solve your problem. He might even wash the dishes himself.

Maybe you're tempted to tell him how to invest because you're anticipating a long future together and hoping the two of you will be able to fund a romantic honeymoon. You wouldn't be looking forward to marrying him, though, if you didn't think he was smart and capable. So instead of underhandedly criticizing his choices, remind yourself that he knows what he's doing. Focus on expressing your desire by saying, "I want to go to Hawaii for our honeymoon."

But what if he really is bad with money and doesn't diversify? Shouldn't you teach him what you know? You'll probably be sorely tempted to, but I don't recommend it. We're talking about *his* money, which you have no claim to. If he loses money because he invests unwisely, he'll learn what to do differently next time.

The most important reason to keep your suggestions to yourself is that telling him he's doing something wrong is disrespectful, and disrespect is an enemy to intimacy. The point of being in a relationship is not so someone can prevent your mistakes by warning you about them, but to support each other even though you're still learning. Therefore, if you'd rather hold hands and snuggle together than argue about the best way to earn a good return, focus on your own life.

## MEN RARELY INITIATE DIVORCE

When a marriage has soured, it's almost always the wife who initiates the divorce. The good news for women is that this means that when you get married, you'll likely have the opportunity to make your marriage work, no matter how bad things get, because he probably won't end the marriage. Most women are surprised when I tell them this because we tend to hear that divorce is rampant, not that wives are the ones who decide to call it quits 90 percent of the time. Since surrendering preserves intimacy, which makes a marriage strong, and you are surrendering from the start of the relationship, the probability that you'll have to get divorced is remote.

My experience with thousands of wives in troubled marriages gave me some insight into this statistic. One of the things I would commonly hear from women in second marriages is that in their first marriage they had to do everything—right up to filing for the divorce. Once they learned about surrendering, however, they realized that they had controlled everything about the union, including when it would end.

Although I had considered divorce at one point, too, I don't think my husband ever did. In fact, when reporters have asked him why he stayed married to me when I was so controlling to begin with, he shrugs and tells them, "It wasn't all that bad." I suspect that his loyalty caused him to overlook my shortcomings while I was scrutinizing his.

There is a proven way to transform even the loneliest marriage into the union you always dreamed was possible. That means you can date with confidence that when you commit to the man who's right for you, you'll be able to stay married till death do you part.

You have that power—and that responsibility.

## Only Happily Married People Can Give You Good Relationship Advice

> ***There is nothing nobler or more admirable than when two people who see eye to eye keep house as man and wife, confounding their enemies and delighting their friends.***
>
> —**Homer**

So how do you cultivate the habits that are so important to ensuring you and your love will grow old together happily? It certainly helps to have the support of another woman who can offer encouragement and feedback.

Some women are able to rely on their mothers for support, but if you've watched your parents separate or become distant, you can't expect your mother to have good advice for you. Even if your parents had a wonderful marriage, the recipe might not have been handed down to you—or may not fit your modern life.

It's not easy to cull the wheat from the chaff among your friends either. Singles certainly can't tell you how to find peace and passion in matrimony, nor can unhappily married friends. Since marriages portrayed in movies or books aren't shackled by the limitations of reality, they aren't accurate pictures of wedded bliss, either.

You might think that you'll also learn what *not* to do by watching unhappy couples, but that doesn't work. For one thing, unhappy couples are uninspiring and may bring out your own fears. Besides, there are so many ways to make a relationship miserable and really only a few simple behaviors that make it wonderful. It makes sense to learn the short list.

The best way to find what you seek is to find a married woman who has the kind of relationship you are looking for. Ask this woman to be your marriage mentor.

You probably know a woman who has a marriage you admire—one where she and her husband laugh together, hold each other in high esteem, and show physical affection. These are the outward signs of an intimate connection. Any woman who has that kind of marriage will be able to give you sage advice about dating, right up to saying "I do." If you're feeling insecure and the temptation to control him is strong, talk to your marriage mentor. She'll be able to give you reality checks, assuage your fears, and tell you about the bliss ahead.

The best way to stay on the right track is to ask the happiest wife you know for her help.

# 22

# TRUST HIS CAPABILITIES

*Every man I meet is in some way my superior.*

—Ralph Waldo Emerson

*The man in your life wants to know that you will respect his decisions, ideas, and tastes even if you don't agree with them. That means that you would refrain from criticizing, dismissing, or demeaning him. You won't try to teach him anything, even if you think you know better, because it's a form of control. Instead, you trust that he's smart and capable.*

*The man who's right for you won't need rescuing: He doesn't need you to put him through school, take care of his kids, let him live at your house. He wants you because he wants a friend and a lover, not a therapist or another mother. The more you trust him, the more he will feel a fierce responsibility not to let you down.*

## Ask Not What You Can Do for Your Boyfriend

The comic strip *Mother Goose & Grimm* once showed Grimm (a dog) on a date with a poodle who was constantly warning him about upcoming curbs, poles, or fire hydrants. At the end of the strip, Grimm rolls his eyes and says, "That's the last time I go out with a seeing-eye dog!"

Like Grimm, most guys don't need a woman to look out for them. In fact, nobody likes to be nagged about being careful. Colin probably didn't much like it when he announced to his girlfriend, Joan, that he'd bought a motorcycle and she reacted by saying, "I don't want anything bad to happen to you."

Granted, motorcycles can be dangerous, but by making the assumption that Colin's new purchase would result in his injury or death, Joan revealed that she didn't trust Colin's ability to keep himself safe. She missed a chance to be excited and happy along with him about his new purchase.

The more comfortable you get in your relationship, the more tempted you will be to behave like Joan and the seeing-eye poodle.

Surrender.

Pessimism, distrust, caretaking, and badgering are forms of control sure to wear you out and dampen passion. This is the time to focus on trusting that he can take care of himself and respecting him by honoring the decisions he makes for his life.

# The Right Man for You Won't Need Rescuing

> *The supreme happiness in life is the conviction that we are loved—loved for ourselves, or rather, loved in spite of ourselves.*
>
> —Victor Hugo

Danielle complained that the only men she attracted were losers who were looking for surrogate mothers. But Danielle's contribution to that equation was that she was constantly offering to help the men she met. When one was floundering in his career, she offered to teach him how to get started in real estate. Another guy didn't have time to buy presents during the holidays, so she did his Christmas shopping for him. Another one was constantly depressed, so she tried to help him through his hard times. In the end, Danielle always felt taken advantage of, even though she was the one who had offered to help. And no wonder. What she was really trying to do was control the men she helped by molding them into the partner she wished for.

"I'm just trying to be nice and hoping that they'll reciprocate," she told me. "But they turn out to be bottomless pits of need." And they didn't respond to her efforts to mold them the way she hoped they would, either.

Fortunately, there are lots of wonderful single men who want to see you for reasons having nothing to do with typing their résumés and watching their kids. The way to stop attracting emotionally or financially needy men is to stop offering to take care of them.

Constantly giving to or doing for a man can wear you out

quickly, because instead of taking care of just your life, which is demanding enough, you're now taking care of two lives. You're in danger of compromising your own self-care and getting cranky when you take the spotlight off of your own activities and happiness to focus on his. If the half hour you would have spent curled up on the couch with a book is gone because you picked up his dry cleaning, you're going to miss your downtime and feel stress.

Helping a man—even if he always seems to ask for it—is an intimacy killer. Think of how smothered you'd feel if your mom came over and cleaned your house while you were out. Sure, you'd be grateful, but you'd also feel a little invaded and reduced to a childlike state. Men feel the same way when we assess their lives, find an area that's lacking, and then attack it as if we were weeding the garden.

Focusing your time and energy on helping him is emasculating. Without saying a word, you imply that he's not capable of running his life by himself, or at least that you don't approve of the way he's doing it. However subtle, the judgment in an apparently kind offer like "Let me help you shop for new clothes," loosely translates to "You don't even know how to dress properly." Yes, you're offering to do something nice, but you're criticizing him at the same time.

In addition to feeling emasculated, sometimes a man will react defensively to offers to dust his apartment, stock his refrigerator, or run to the post office. He senses that there will be a price to pay at some point. For instance, Vicky was always doing something thoughtful for Phil, like bringing him something she baked, buying him new bath towels, and taking his car to be washed. Vicky was, by nature, generous and enjoyed giving, but Phil didn't seem to take pleasure in all the receiving. "After a while, he would actually say, 'Stop giving me things, okay?' " Vicky recalled. "I was offended because that's the kind of person I am. That's one of the things everybody likes about me."

On further reflection, Vicky realized that in addition to her giving nature, she had an ulterior motive for showering Phil with gifts: "If I'm really honest, I have to admit that I gave him things to make sure he wouldn't stop liking me," she realized sadly. "I wanted him to owe me so that he couldn't leave me so easily."

Phil did break up with Vicky, and although she was devastated, she learned an important lesson. "I don't want to try to make people like me by giving them things anymore," she told me. She realized that she no longer had to quell her fear that she was unlovable by bestowing gifts and favors on a man. "It's just one more way that I've tried to control my relationships. It's sad that I didn't think anyone would like me if I wasn't doing something for them or giving them things, but that's what part of me believed."

Cheryl's situation was a little different because although she was doing lots of favors for her boyfriend Bill initially, she wasn't enjoying it. But *he* was. When she decided to stop doing so much for him and simply focus on her self-care, the relationship deteriorated quickly. "I think he was looking for a mother-type, which I don't want to be," she said. "Turning my attention to self-care made it very obvious that we weren't going to be happy together, so we broke up. It's actually a relief."

## Control Disguised as a Gift Is Still Control

*Growth demands a temporary surrender of security.*

—Gail Sheehy

Vicky's former modus operandi is not unusual. I frequently see women who seem overly eager to throw elaborate birthday parties for their boyfriends, spend more than they can afford on Christmas gifts, and clean their apartments from top to bottom even though they've had a hectic work week. It's hard to find fault with such women—or understand why their boyfriends grow agitated and distant—unless you understand the nature of control. If a woman's motive for such generosity is to try to make him like her more or feel he owes her something, he'll know it and feel a corresponding drop in affection because she wants to mold him.

Instead of sacrificing your time and money for a man, a much better path to nurturing affection is to treat a man with respect by honoring his choices—whether that's a candy bar for lunch, a disheveled room, or taking three aspirins when the bottle says to take two.

When you feel the temptation to pick up something nutritious for him, straighten up his place, or monitor his painkillers, you're supervising a grown man, and that is both unnecessary and unattractive.

## Thank Goodness for Small Favors

The man who is right for you will want your respect *more* than your guidance or your help running errands. And trusting the man you admire to solve his own problems is a wonderful way to show respect.

I'm not suggesting that you wouldn't help a man who asked you to—to a point. For instance, if he asks you to pick him up because his car stalled and you're able to do it without making yourself a stress case, then by all means do it. If he's sick and asks you to bring over some food, that's a great opportunity to show your affection. The difference here is:

- He's asking, as opposed to you offering.
- It's something you can do without feeling resentful later.
- It's a one-time event, not an ongoing commitment such as doing his laundry every week or putting him through medical school.

The problem with committing to ongoing favors is that you lose the chance to assess your energy stores each time to determine if you can complete the task without becoming resentful. Worse still, you put yourself in a bad spot, because the only way out of doing the favor is to retract your offer. Now, instead of getting credit for doing something thoughtful if you do the favor, you're letting him down when you don't. Now you feel guilty for *not* doing something nice for him, which stinks.

But what if you're dating a man who is in transition, going back to school, or struggling? You may be tempted to lighten his load, but when you do, you step out of the realm of girlfriend and into the realm of benefactor, which will have a detrimental effect on the romance. If you're shouldering all the rent or working to pay his tuition, you'll feel more like a mother than a girlfriend. He'll feel less attraction to a woman who reminds him of his mother. Plus, since you're just dating, there's no promise that the sacrifices you make now will benefit you in the future. The stories of couples who break up after she put him through medical school are rampant. Consider them a warning.

Finally, he doesn't need your help to accomplish his goals, especially if he started reaching for them before he met you.

## YOU CAN STILL RESPECT THINGS YOU DON'T APPROVE OF

Sometimes one man's fun is his girlfriend's nightmare. For instance, Michael couldn't wait to show Elaine pictures from his family's Independence Day celebration. Elaine could tell her boyfriend was very proud and excited for her to see the pictures, so she was horrified when he told her the story of how his cousin had brought illegal fireworks to the party and Michael had lit them and nearly burned down the neighborhood. The *pièce de résistance* of his photo collection was a snapshot of his old granny—who was too frail to move—sitting in a chair that had holes on both sides of her where balls of flame had shot through the fabric.

"I didn't approve of what he had done," Elaine said, "so I wasn't going to say I thought it was great. But I could tell he was excited to show me, and I didn't want to crush him, so I said nothing."

Michael wasn't looking for Elaine's approval. He just wanted to share his misadventures with her for the fun of it. Elaine mistakenly thought she was in a position to influence his future behavior. "I was thinking, 'I don't ever want him to do that again because it's too dangerous,' so I withheld any reaction that he might have taken as encouragement." Her lack of reaction was meant to control his behavior, but the end result was that she missed out on a chance to connect with him and laugh about his misadventure.

Once you become part of a couple, it's easy to fall into the trap of holding your beau to higher standards than you would a close friend. To gain perspective, ask yourself if you would be that hard on a pal in that same situation and adjust your measuring stick accordingly.

When Elaine considered how she would have reacted if a friend had shown her the same pictures, she admitted that she probably would have teased the friend by saying, "So that's how you get your kicks, huh?" The difference being that she didn't feel compelled to try to control what a friend would do.

## Maintaining Mutual Attraction

> *If this world affords true happiness, it is to be found in a home where love and confidence increase with the years.*
>
> —A. Edward Newton

If you stop controlling, criticizing, rescuing, or helping a man, something amazing happens: You maintain the intimacy and connection you felt when you first discovered your mutual attraction. That's because he can continue to spend his energy trying to please you instead of defending himself against you, and you can continue to spend your energy practicing good self-care instead of trying to control him. When you respect your boyfriend, there's little to argue about, so bickering and full-blown fights are rare. Your boyfriend will be grateful for your faith in him, and that gratitude will manifest as more hand-holding, romantic dinners, and laughing together.

# 23

# EXPRESS YOUR HURT WITHOUT MAKING DEMANDS

*We are more often frightened than hurt; and we suffer more from imagination than from reality.*

—Lucius Annaeus Seneca

*Before you tell your boyfriend that you're hurt about something he did or didn't do, examine your expectations. If you're hurt because he didn't offer to drive, wanted to watch the game on Friday night instead of seeing you, or hasn't called since Tuesday, you may be trying to force your agenda on the relationship.*

*If, on the other hand, you're hurt because you feel criticized, even indirectly, respond by saying "Ouch!" Resist the urge to use your verbal skills to threaten or wound him.*

## Let Go of Your Agenda

We each have a mental picture of how a long-term relationship should start out, and anything that falls short of that makes us nervous. As soon as we feel that anxiety, the urge to control kicks in. One of the ways we unwittingly try to control men is by telling them that we're hurt when they don't do things our way. Pulling at their heartstrings by playing the pain card is yet another way of trying to make them change. Instead, it makes them recoil.

Think very carefully before you tell your boyfriend you're hurt because of something he *didn't* do that you think he should have. What you're really doing is enforcing your agenda.

In your perfect world, your boyfriend knows just how to behave. He says and does what you want him to. His timing is impeccable. In reality, of course, his behavior, tone, and timing sometimes seem strange. Part of being intimate is letting go of your expectations and accepting that his way isn't wrong or meant to hurt you. You can't program him like a robot, but you don't want a robot anyway. Because he's human, he may do something that disappoints you from time to time.

Your pain may feel very real, but it's based on the assumption that he should act according to the predetermined scenario that plays in your head. With that premise, you will constantly be let down. Your boyfriend will grow increasingly frustrated as he realizes that he can't meet your unspoken expectations and being himself isn't good enough.

## Overlook "Sins" of Omission

> *When you love someone, all your saved-up wishes start coming out.*
>
> —Elizabeth Bowen

Maybe you're hurt that he hasn't asked you out for the following weekend, hasn't invited you to meet his parents yet, or hasn't called you as much as you wish he would. You might be tempted to say, "I'm hurt that you didn't invite me to meet your parents." Or, worse, you might express your disappointment by giving him the silent treatment or acting glum.

Before you do, consider your expectations.

For instance, it may seem logical to you that he should invite you to meet his parents six weeks after you start dating. You could tell him as much. But surrendering means leaving the timing of that meeting to him.

Telling him that you're hurt that he hasn't done something—such as dressed up more to meet your parents or cleaned out his car before he picked you up—is controlling. Yes, you may be hurt, but what you're really expressing—and what he hears—is that you want the course of events to play out differently so that the relationship can progress to the next level or look the way you imagined it would. When you do that, you're no longer enjoying the magic and adventure of a close connection.

Judy was feeling attached to Tom after they had been dating for two months, so she was nervous when he stopped calling as much. "He only calls maybe once or twice a day, instead of several times a day like he did before," she told me. "Is it because he's not interested anymore? Can't I just be straightforward and ask him if he's still interested?"

While Judy considered her question "straightforward," it was actually manipulative. On the one hand, she was hoping Tom would respond by saying, "Yes, I'm still interested and I'm sorry I haven't called as much. From now on, I'll call you at least three times every day." On the other hand, she told herself that if he wasn't interested anymore, she wanted to know now so she could stop feeling so vulnerable. She wanted to force him to make a decision about the future of the relationship to assuage her fear of abandonment.

The problem with forcing his hand is that nobody likes to be cornered. No matter how much Tom wanted to continue to see Judy at that moment, he probably would have been too put off by her implied criticism to say anything reassuring.

As we talked, Judy admitted that Tom had been very busy with work for the past few days, which coincided with his calls becoming less frequent. She also acknowledged that he still seemed happy to talk to her when he did call. Finally, Judy realized that she had been so absorbed in him and wondering whether he would call that she had abandoned herself. Instead of meditating one morning, she replayed his previous phone messages to look for clues as to how he was feeling. Instead of lunching with friends, she left herself open in case he wanted to meet. Missing out on the things she normally did to rejuvenate herself left Judy feeling drained and unhappy. The more miserable she felt, the more she was tempted to focus on when Tom was ever going to call and make her feel better.

"I'm just hurt that he doesn't want to talk to me as much," Judy said when she started focusing on herself and how she was feeling. "But I know that's because I want to control him."

On further reflection, Judy discovered a much more vulnerable sentiment than "I'm hurt that you don't call me as much." A more risky, but more honest, message would be to tell Tom that she missed him.

Saying "I miss you" beautifully expressed how Judy felt without criticizing or trying to make Tom behave differently.

Sometimes women are afraid to say those words to a man because they worry it will make him think that she's getting too serious or pressuring him. But "I miss you" doesn't make any such demands. It's a pure expression of what you feel, not what you expect him to do. Everyone likes to be missed, but it can be hard to say those words when you're trying to protect yourself by seeming nonchalant.

| SITUATION | CONTROLLING RESPONSE | SURRENDERED RESPONSE |
|---|---|---|
| **You want more time together.** | **"You don't make me a priority in your life."** | **"I miss you."** |
| **He makes fun of how you dance.** | **"You're so rude!"** | **"Ouch!"** |
| **He doesn't invite you to his work party** | **"I'm hurt that you didn't invite me."** | **Check your expectations and say nothing. Practice self-care!** |

## WHEN YOU'RE HURT, SAY "OUCH!"

There may be times that your boyfriend hurts your feelings by snapping at you, criticizing you, or telling you how to do something. Unlike the disappointment you feel when he falls short of your expectations, this stings because it pierces your spirit.

At these times, you might be tempted to strike back or to engage him in a discussion that will most likely end up escalating into a fight.

Here's another idea. Stay collected, but say "Ouch!" to let him know you're hurt. This is a powerful way of letting him know that you're injured without engaging in a battle or insulting him back.

I know it sounds crazy to lay down your arms just when you're feeling attacked. However, saying "ouch" is a good way to tell him that he struck a nerve without going on the offense yourself. Saying "ouch" feels vulnerable, because in that moment you may feel like you're pointing out your weak spots to the enemy when you'd prefer to seem invincible. But he's not the enemy, and being vulnerable will help remind both of you that you're on the same team. Admitting you're stung won't make you seem oversensitive, but it will give him the chance to make amends.

You might think you're letting him off the hook too easily if he somehow insults you and you don't respond in kind. But if you're trying to nurture intimacy, responding with a clever comeback would leave you both hurt, more guarded, and less likely to relax and enjoy each other's company. Bickering before you've established a solid emotional bond is a sure way to end the romance before it's begun. You will also feel a loss of dignity when you hear yourself say something biting, which in turn could cause you to doubt how desirable you are. It's hard to feel attractive and feminine when you just laid somebody low.

If you're seeing a guy who hurts you so regularly that you're saying "ouch" every time you're together, that's a big red flag that he's probably not the right guy for you. A man who can't refrain from insulting you—even inadvertently—is not the right man for you.

## Sins of Omission vs. Sins of Commission

*Willfulness must give way to willingness and surrender. Mastery must yield to mystery.*

—Gerald G. May

Is your desire to express your hurt manipulation? You can find out once you establish whether you're feeling pain because of something he *did* do or say or because of something he *didn't* do or say. Responding to a sharp or unkind comment with hurt is appropriate. However, saying "ouch" because he didn't bring you flowers is about forcing your agenda.

Many women tell me that they feel awkward saying "ouch" and that they would rather say that they feel hurt and explain why. For instance:

"When you grabbed the spatula out of my hand, I was upset because it seems like you think you know better than I do when to flip the pancakes."

"I was hurt when you snapped at me, because I don't like to be yelled at."

"You hurt my feelings when you said I never let you do what you want."

You could certainly say any of those things and be completely justified in doing so. However, each sentence carries an implied accusation or criticism of him. "You think you're better than I am"; "You yelled at me"; "Your perspective is unreasonable."

By comparison, saying "ouch" is strictly about you. When you criticize someone, it's only natural for him to respond defensively. When you feel defensive, it's much harder to hear the voice of your own conscience. Once your boyfriend feels defensive, he may try to justify his behavior. It isn't right or fair, but it's human. Now you're engaged in a fight about whether what he said or did was okay. Suddenly your hurt is no longer the topic of discussion, so nobody is happy. By contrast, using the simple, small word "ouch" keeps the focus of the conversation squarely where it belongs without fueling a battle.

You'll be tempted to go on and explain, but there's no need, because that single word describes your hurt perfectly. Saying "ouch" is scary, but it's a powerful way to indicate to the man you're with that you deserve to be treated tenderly.

If you say "ouch" because your beau didn't do something that you would have liked—call it a "sin" of omission—he would have no idea what you were talking about. So another way to decide whether or not to express hurt is to ask yourself if you have something to say "ouch" *in response to.* If not, then you're trying to enforce your agenda, and you're better off letting life surprise you.

## Make a Deal with Yourself

> *I first learned the concepts of nonviolence in my marriage.*
>
> —Mahatma Gandhi

You'll probably feel scared and vulnerable and feel like running away at times in your relationship. When you do, you'll be tempted to break up, call it off, and move on. Instead, make a deal with yourself that you must consistently want to break up with your man for at least one full week before you follow through. If on Wednesday you want to break up and on Sunday you realize you love him again and by the following Wednesday you hate him again, that doesn't count. You have to be consistent for the whole week. A week is not that long in the great scheme of a love relationship, but it can seem unbearable when you're terrified and trying to run away.

I'm not suggesting that you stop seeing him for a week and then decide what to do. Carry on with romance as usual and use the opportunity to confront your own fears. Many women don't realize that *threatening* to break up when you don't mean it is verbally abusive. The only time you need to say, "I'm leaving you," is when you are about to walk away for good. That's it.

Stay the course of a Surrendered Single and you will avoid the ugliness of controlling through on-again-off-again behavior.

# 24

# KEEP YOUR LIFE EVEN THOUGH HE'S IN IT

*There is an important difference between love and friendship. While the former delights in extremes and opposites, the latter demands equality.*

—FRANÇOISE D'AUBIGNÉ DE MAINTENON

*Once you meet a new man, you may be tempted to spend less time with friends or doing the activities that were a part of your life before you met him. Instead of sacrificing everything else you enjoy so you can spend all your time with him, remember that no one person can meet all of your emotional needs. Casting aside friends and hobbies that you once enjoyed in favor of total immersion with a man could make you cranky and miserable, which is not attractive.*

*Keeping the trappings of your pre-boyfriend days will help you maintain balance in your life, which means you'll be happier. The happier and more balanced you are, the healthier the relationship will be.*

# Falling in Love Is Time-Consuming

> *The moment you have in your heart this extraordinary thing called love and feel the depth, the delight, the ecstasy of it, you will discover that for you the world is transformed.*
>
> —J. Krishnamurti

When you're in the early stages of a relationship, it's natural to pull back from some of your other activities and relationships. You'll want to spend every waking moment with him, and that means bumping your best friend, your sister, and your yoga class into lower slots on your list of priorities. When the romance is new, nothing else compares to the exhilaration and electricity you feel when you're with him.

But before you cancel everything that was on your calendar, start staying up too late to keep up with him, and make "All You Need Is Love" your anthem, remember that keeping yourself balanced and happy is critical for a successful intimate relationship. If the things you're tempted to cross off your calendar are things that used to contribute to your sense of well-being, consider keeping them in your schedule. No great love was ever founded on one person giving up the things she loved and enjoyed.

If yoga was helping you stay serene when work was stressful, you're setting yourself up for a fall if you stop going. If you're not getting enough sleep because you stay up late to talk to your boyfriend, you will soon find yourself ragged and ill-tempered. If having solitude helps you clear your head and you're always with him, you won't be your best self for long.

To bring your best self to your romantic relationship, give yourself what you need every day.

## A Good Guy Will Support Your Self-Care

Of course you won't talk to your girlfriends as much, but don't forget about them entirely. Keep up your karate lessons, go on the vacation you planned without him, and get the rest you need, even if it means telling him you can't see him for one night. A good guy will support you in doing what makes you happy, even if it means he has to wait to be with you.

Jillian struggled with this when she and Alan had been dating for only two months. She had plans to go out to dinner with two girlfriends on Friday night when he called at the last minute and invited her to a Stevie Nicks concert. Naturally, Jillian was sorely tempted to cancel on her friends and take the opportunity to go with her new love, especially since she was afraid that rejecting him might make him go away. Instead, she made the difficult decision to stick to her original plan, mostly because she would have felt guilty about canceling on her friends. On another level, Jillian may have realized that the chatter and laughter of girlfriends was exactly what she needed at that moment.

With all the excitement of meeting Alan, Jillian hadn't had a girls' night out in a while. She didn't want to lose the connection with her pals. She loved having someplace to compare notes about her love life and get advice on how much to dress up for an upcoming work party. Granted, Jillian could have talked to Alan about any of those topics, but connecting with other feminine spirits gives our lives more abundance and dimension. Just as yoga can be relaxing and stabilizing, so being with women reminds us that we are women, which is important to a healthy relationship.

Choosing to spend time with her girlfriends instead of accepting Alan's offer didn't make him feel any less important, nor did it quell his interest. She was relieved when Alan responded tenderly and supported her in not disappointing her friends. "I guess this means you won't cancel on me at the last minute, so that's nice to know about you."

Having missed his chance to be with her that night, Alan was probably even more eager to see her next time.

Your boyfriend will also support your decision—even when it means being apart—if he knows you're with girlfriends, taking time for yourself, napping, or doing anything else that will make you happy.

# 25

# BECOMING YOUR BEST SELF WILL BRING OUT THE BEST IN HIM

*Few things are harder to put up with than*
*the annoyance of a good example.*
—MARK TWAIN

***While you can't change anyone other than yourself, you can set a positive tone for the relationship. Instead of pointing out his faults, hold a mirror up to his strengths.***

***Be the first to show appreciation and vulnerability, and he will respond in kind. Just as we tend to exercise more when we're with an active friend and drink more when we're with a friend who likes to party, being around someone who is generous, accepting, and grateful brings out those qualities in us, too.***

## How to Win Friends and Influence People You Love

> *Gratitude unlocks the fullness of life. It turns what we have into enough, and more. It turns denial into acceptance, chaos to order, confusion to clarity. It can turn a meal into a feast, a house into a home, a stranger into a friend.*
>
> —Melody Beattie

Michelle was resentful toward her live-in boyfriend, Zack, because she felt he didn't appreciate her efforts to keep their apartment orderly and make sure the refrigerator contained more than just condiments. This issue came up in my workshop when the homework assignment was to express gratitude for Zack three times every day for a week. "Why should I act like I'm grateful for what he does when he isn't grateful for what I do? Plus, I do more than him anyway," she objected.

But Michelle had already told us that Zack gave her spontaneous neck rubs, took her to dinner frequently, and changed the oil in her car whenever it needed it. Clearly, he was generous and giving, but Michelle didn't see it that way because she felt so overburdened with taking care of the house and doing the bulk of the cooking. In her mind, because he wasn't helping with the things that *she* really wanted help with, he wasn't helping at all. As a result, she was stingy with her thanks.

Zack seemed withdrawn, which is not surprising, since his kindnesses were never acknowledged. Perhaps he was even afraid to thank her because he feared that he might get a critical response like, "At least you appreciate that I do everything around here!"

Granted, it's hard to be grateful when you feel alone with your responsibilities, but worrying about what she lacked instead of focusing on how much Zack gave her skewed Michelle's perspective. Instead of recognizing his contributions and gifts, she saw only his faults.

The point of the gratitude exercise was to demonstrate that although we can't always change our circumstances, we can change our attitude. I wanted Michelle to see that she could improve the picture by making a decision to see her life as a glass half-full instead of half-empty. Expressing gratitude has the magical quality of making our circumstances seem brighter.

Despite her objections to the assignment, Michelle agreed to try being generous with her gratitude for the week just as an experiment. She found three things to thank him for every day. Halfway through the week, she discovered another fringe benefit to her behavior when Zack pleasantly surprised her by saying, "You've really taught me that we need to appreciate each other more. I want to thank you for making dinner tonight."

"That was something I always wanted to hear from him, that he appreciated what I did. I just loved it. But maybe even more importantly, expressing my gratitude every day also made *me* appreciate him more. He really does a lot for me that I take for granted," Michelle said.

Michelle's focus for this exercise was to improve her own outlook, not to make her boyfriend thank her. It so happens that her efforts to become her best self affected the culture of their relationship. Although she didn't prompt him to say he appreciated her making dinner, she did set an example that he quickly followed. Instead of focusing on how Zack didn't appreciate her (which she couldn't do anything about anyway), Michelle looked at her own behavior and became willing to change. Not only did she make progress toward becoming her best self, she brought the entire relationship to higher ground.

That's what surrendering is all about.

## All Life Is a Mirror

> *Everything that irritates us about others can lead us to an understanding of ourselves.*
>
> —Carl Jung

Becoming your best self will have a positive impact on the man who's committed to you.

Just as a kid is more prone to grabbing someone else's toy after a playmate takes his, adults are highly susceptible to others' behavior. We tend to gossip when we're with friends who love to dish dirt, eat junk food when we're with ice cream–loving pals, and spend too much when we shop with shopaholics. Part of human nature is that we influence each other—for better or worse.

This is not to say that you can improve everything about your boyfriend by improving yourself. For instance, if you think he needs to lose a little weight, you won't necessarily see him exercising more because you've decided to go to a gym regularly. If it's his table manners that bother you, even being really diligent about chewing with your mouth closed is not going to reform him. However, making a decision to be more accepting will reverberate in a positive way.

For one thing, working to keep only your side of the street clean will keep you from engaging in criticism that leads to bickering or distance. Here's what I mean: If you find his table manners appalling, you can either say something critical (because there's no way to correct his table manners without criticizing him) or recognize that you too have imperfections and accept his quirks.

If you decide to criticize him, there's no guarantee that he'll improve the way he behaves, but you'll certainly lose the harmony and intimacy you might have shared. Let's say he feels defensive and unconsciously retaliates by criticizing your driving. That isn't right and it isn't fair, but it is human.

Or maybe he withdraws a bit, and you wonder why he's so quiet or uninterested in conversation with you. You're certainly not responsible for his behavior, but you have a part in creating a culture where the two of you demean each other or become distant.

You're not responsible for what anyone else does, but you can do your part to set a supportive tone by working to improve only yourself.

## People Need Love Most When They're the Most Unlovable

In my twenties I was a singer in a rock band that had just gotten its first big break: a chance to open for the Wild Colonials, who had a hit song at the time. I was excited, nervous, and unprepared when I called the club to make arrangements with the stage crew for our act. Sam, the stage manager, had no patience for me. By the time we hung up, his harsh words about how unprofessional I was and how unlikely our band was to succeed had me in tears. At the next rehearsal, I told the rest of the band they should watch out for Sam because he would be very difficult to work with. The bass player wisely suggested that we "kill him with kindness" instead.

"What?" I argued incredulously. "There's no way I'm going to be nice to him after what he said to me!"

Still, the bass player insisted that probably nobody was nice to Sam and that he just needed some appreciation. Anxious to have our big show go well, I decided that I would make an effort to befriend Sam. I thought of something I could authentically thank him for: his referral to a good videographer to tape our performance. I also made him brownies. I gave him my gratitude and the baked goods at the same time, and the curmudgeonly stage manager was so taken aback he looked like he was going to cry.

After that, Sam quickly got to work devising spectacular lighting for our set and telling me his best show tips. By the time we performed, I could see this man had a heart of gold under his cantankerous exterior.

Your boyfriend probably is not as curmudgeonly as Sam, but he may get irritable from time to time. When he does, it can't hurt to remember that he needs your love and acceptance more than he does when he's pleasant and upbeat. You may worry, as I have before, that treating a man with such generosity when he's behaving like a boor will reinforce negative behavior.

It turns out, just the opposite is true.

The more you behave maturely, the more he'll feel embarrassed about being childish for two reasons: first, that you're not giving him any fuel for his fire and, second, because of the uncomfortable contrast between your actions and his.

Sure it's tempting to complain or to be a brat right back, but when I've been big enough to be my best self even when my husband isn't his best self, he tends to come around quickly.

## Your Best Self Reinforces the Positive

> *Nothing is so aggravating than calmness.*
> —Oscar Wilde

If you're constantly reflecting back something negative to your boyfriend—like "you're irresponsible" or "you always make a mess"—you're going to feel like your worst self, not your best. When I said to my husband, "You're chewing with your mouth open again," or "You always lose your keys," I felt like a shrew and not the supportive, kind person I wanted to be.

Indulging in such negative comments emasculates the man you love. Since he knows that you know him better than anyone else, he's likely to give your words a lot of weight. Over time your persistent messages will permeate his thoughts, become his belief, and affect how he behaves—and not for the better.

While it's common for women to have regular intimate talks with girlfriends, men tend to talk most confidentially with the woman in their lives. So while you're getting feedback and opinions from several people who know you well, your boyfriend may be hearing your opinion exclusively on the most personal details in his life. Therefore, what men see reflected back to them from the woman who knows them best in the world colors their view of themselves.

If, on the other hand, you can authentically say, "You're so good with computers," or "You're so generous," you reinforce something positive, and that helps foster a positive outlook. Now you are behaving your best, which feels good. Since *I* feel better when I'm upbeat and encouraging to John, rather than demeaning and critical, reinforcing his gifts rather than his faults is an important part of being my best self.

As a fringe benefit, my compliments will also impact his thoughts and behavior and make him feel stronger.

Sometimes women fear that reinforcing a man's talents or gifts is dangerous. At times, he may appear self-absorbed or unaffected by your comments. But humans are fragile, and everybody needs positive reinforcement, especially from the person they love the most. Appreciating a man won't make him feel superior or become an egomaniac, but it will make him feel more secure in the relationship and in the world, which is a wonderful gift to give him. You may feel vulnerable doing this, but as long as your words are genuine, you have nothing to be embarrassed or worried about. Let go of how he responds. Even if he seems uncomfortable with your nice comments, you can say them with confidence as part of becoming your best self.

If this sounds like manipulation, remember that there's a big difference between simply expressing appreciation for someone's gifts and trying to get him to improve what he eats or how he dresses. Expressing gratitude and praise freely gives you an optimistic glow and a warm feeling, which is why it's worth doing. It doesn't hurt to know that it also has a positive effect on those around you.

This approach has proved much more satisfying than trying—and failing—to change my husband. It also contributes to a wonderful romance in which we support and bring out the best in each other.

### What to Do When a Man Is Moody

Let's say your boyfriend is unresponsive, swearing loudly, or responding tersely. What can you do to snap him out of it? Nothing. John Gray, author of *Men Are from Mars, Women Are from Venus,* talks about how men will go in their caves from time to time and that it's best if women let them stay there until they've worked things out. Think of a man who's out of sorts as one who has gone into his cave, even if he hasn't gone anywhere.

Sure, it's tempting to say, "What's wrong?" or tell him he's in a bad mood, but starting a conversation like that is a setup for disaster, since he's obviously not feeling his best. What he needs is acceptance, and lots of it, and what you need is to get busy doing something distracting and enjoyable. This is a way of taking care of yourself while also demonstrating that you trust him to solve his problems even if the process looks messy.

His behavior may sound like a cry for help to you, but you're not Florence Nightingale, the Red Cross, or his therapist. It's not your job to make him feel better or fix whatever problem he's having. Trust that if he needs your help, he'll ask for it. If he doesn't ask, then trying to help him is intruding in a way that has more to do with wanting to control him so you don't have to feel uncomfortable than it does with wanting to lighten his load.

His foul mood will pass, and likely pass more quickly if you leave him to his own devices.

# 26

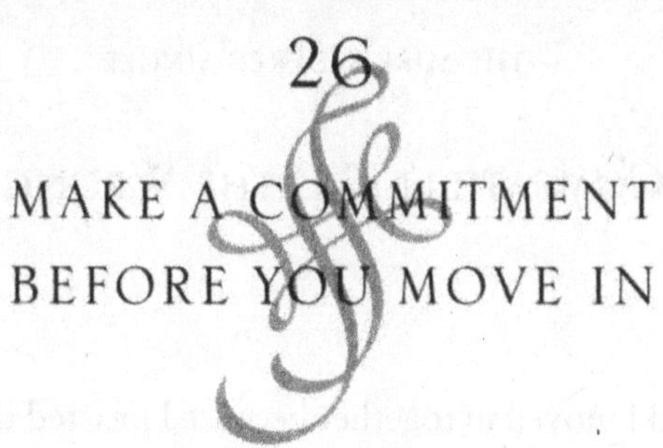

# MAKE A COMMITMENT BEFORE YOU MOVE IN

*Chains do not hold a marriage together. It is threads, hundreds of tiny threads which sew people together through the years. That is what makes a marriage last—more than passion or even sex!*

—SIMONE SIGNORET

*Keep your own place until you have a formal commitment so that you can be certain you're willing and wanting to forge a life with him.*

*Commitment itself is one of the things that makes love last, so if you want your romance to last a lifetime, live separately until you're ready to say "till death do we part."*

*When you live together, the relationship can be renegotiated at any time, which makes it much more volatile than marriage.*

*Instead of moving in together to "see how it goes," give your relationship a better chance to endure by investing your full faith and trust in your future as a couple. Compatibility is not about whether you irritate each other from time to time, but whether you're willing to hang in and work out your difficulties.*

## "Are We Compatible?" Is the Wrong Question

John and I moved in together because I insisted that sharing the same apartment was more convenient, cut housework in half, and eliminated roommates. My argument was logical, but in truth I pushed the issue because I was desperate to know if John liked me enough to move in with me. I was testing him.

Although I got what I wanted when we moved into a small house together, I knew I had forced him to some degree. I cheated myself out of the pleasure and joy of knowing that he really *wanted* to share a home with me. Looking back, I realize that moving in together was like putting a big Band-Aid over my insecurities about whether John really liked me or not. It also helped me avoid facing my fear that marriage was too dangerous. I decided to control things because I was afraid.

Maybe you feel that living together is the best way to see if the two of you can handle day-to-day challenges without falling apart.

Maybe you're afraid to commit without knowing that you'll be able to work through big disagreements that arise only when you live together: how to raise step-children, whose job takes precedence if one of you must relocate, and how to balance saving and spending. Perhaps you think that moving in together will give you more time to decide if this is the right relationship for you. Or maybe you want to make sure that he's not seeing anyone but you.

However, dating without living together provides plenty of opportunities to practice conflict resolution and determine whether he's your good guy. If you're able to work through disagreements and come out on the other side, then you have proof positive that you can succeed together in matrimony.

The rationale is that moving in together before marriage gives the couple a chance to see if they're compatible. But since every couple is going to have conflict, *Will we be compatible?* is the wrong question. You will certainly have disagreements at times. That doesn't mean you won't also have intimacy, loyalty, and longevity.

Finding out if you're compatible doesn't mean learning whether he leaves his socks on the floor or gets uptight when you leave dishes in the sink. After all, any man you have a romance with will do things that irritate you. Those are tiny problems that every couple has to work through. The real question is, *Will we be willing to stay and work through our differences so that we can continue to enjoy the tenderness, comfort and passion we find together?*

Saying "I do" and getting a legal contract increases the likelihood that you will.

## CONTROL BY ANY OTHER NAME IS STILL CONTROL

> *As your faith is strengthened, you will find that there is no longer the need to have a sense of control, that things will flow as they will, and that you will flow with them, to your great delight and benefit.*
>
> —EMMANUEL

Megan realized after her relationship with Tony ended that she had also pushed to move in together and that her real motivation was to keep tabs on him. "I didn't like not knowing where he was, and I didn't want him to meet someone else," she admitted. She didn't trust that he wanted to be with her, so she tried to control where he was by inviting him to move in. That way, she figured, he could only be with her.

The real issue that Megan should have been focused on was that she felt she couldn't trust him unless they were living together. Instead, she pushed for closer proximity to assuage her fears. But Megan's bid for control was transparent and wore on Tony as she constantly asked him where he was going, when he would be back, and who he was going to see. He grew tired of being treated like a little boy. "Just trust me," he often said. Her tendency to control his every move eventually drove him away.

Shortly after Janet met Ken, he had to move out of his apartment. Janet offered to let him move into her townhouse, thinking he would be able to pull his life together if he lived in a nice environment and had some relief from his financial pressures. Ken said he was trying to find a better job and wanted to pay off his debts, so Janet figured she was giving him that chance. She secretly hoped he would become more financially secure so that they could get married without her having to take on his debts. But Ken wasn't looking very hard for that new job, and she began to feel resentful that he wasn't trying to become the man she wanted him to be. Months later, he still hadn't improved his financial situation one bit.

"I figured if we lived together, he would pick up some better habits," Janet told me. What she really meant is that she hoped she could change him by getting him to earn more money and pay off debts. When she finally got rid of him, Janet felt thoroughly taken advantage of.

Once we were living together, I mentioned to John that we could be on each other's health plans if we were married, and John agreed that it was a good idea. On that completely unromantic note, we got engaged. Once again, I denied myself the opportunity to receive a sweet, heartfelt proposal. I didn't even realize it until my sister-in-law asked how John had asked me to marry him.

Eventually John did get on one knee and tell me he loved me

and wanted me to be his wife, which was wonderful. But it was probably not half as wonderful as what he would have done if I had left the whole thing up to him to begin with. Even worse, my urge to control and my lack of trust in John followed us into the marriage and nearly ruined it.

Had I continued to date John from our separate apartments, I would have gotten a much more gratifying show of love and set a better tone for the whole relationship. We were married for years before I realized how my controlling habits were straining the relationship. When I finally surrendered—mostly as a desperate attempt to save my marriage—I found the rewards of spontaneity, trust, and intimacy far exceeded being able to make things go the way I wanted them.

Megan, Janet, and I would have all said that we had decided to live with our boyfriends because we were in love. In reality, we lived with our boyfriends because we were in fear. I was afraid John wouldn't propose of his own accord, Megan was afraid that Tony would date someone else, and Janet was afraid that Ken couldn't succeed on his own. We each cheated ourselves out of true romance, thoughtfulness, and the sweetness of engaging with a man without trying to control him.

If you're tempted to move in with your boyfriend, examine your feelings to see if you're reacting from desire or fear. One way to get to the truth is to ask yourself if you would marry him right now. There are three possible answers: "yes," "no," and "not yet." If the answer is "yes!" then do your part to honor your desire. If the answer is "no way," then you probably shouldn't even be dating him.

Most likely, the answer is "not yet," and that signals that it's too soon to live together. It's especially dangerous to move in with a man when you're not sure you want to marry him. You make it very difficult to walk away later when you're sharing closets and have two cats together—or when your three-year-old daughter is calling him Daddy.

## Living Together Is Riskier Than Getting Married

> *One advantage of marriage, it seems to me, is that when you fall out of love with him, or he falls out of love with you, it keeps you together until you maybe fall in love again.*
>
> —Judith Viorst

A wedding ceremony—however small and private—is a sacred commitment in front of God and everybody. Moving in together is sneaking in under the radar with the understanding that either of you can renegotiate the status of your relationship at any time.

Both agreements have the potential for joy and heartbreak, but if you're anything like I was, living together probably seems less risky to you. If you just move in together, there's no social pressure—or support—to make your living arrangement work. You won't embarrass your family or yourself if someone has to move out. You won't have to describe the parting with that word that seems synonymous with failure: divorce. That's why simply sending out change-of-address cards may seem safer than wedding invitations.

True, you don't need a lawyer to go your separate ways, but the emotional trauma of losing your relationship and the home you've grown accustomed to is devastating.

## Save Nothing for the Trip Back

In the movie *Gattica,* two brothers compete with each other to see who can swim the farthest out in the ocean before he has to turn back for shore. The younger, stronger brother is shocked when his older brother finally beats him and demands to know how he did it. The weaker but more determined brother tells him, "I saved nothing for the trip back."

Love relationships deserve the same kind of courage and commitment. If you know in your heart you're with a good guy, then you can safely get off the fence and marry him. Moving in without a sacred commitment is a way of withholding a part of yourself that's critical to the success of your union. Instead of saying, "Take all of me," you're message is, "Let's see how it goes." You're holding back your faith, confidence, and conviction, and no relationship will succeed without those.

Of course, the suggestion to live together could come from your boyfriend, in which case you can simply tell him that you wouldn't be comfortable with that arrangement. For one thing, you wouldn't want to give someone you love less than what he deserves in the way of your commitment to him. You wouldn't want to put either of you at such great risk.

Since marriage is a longer-term proposition than living together, it may take you both longer to want to take that step. Therefore, waiting for a greater commitment may take more patience, but it will also be more gratifying and improve your chances of having a successful lifelong romance.

The benefit of getting married before you move in together is that when problems do arise, both of you will share a sense that they can be overcome instead of knowing that there's an escape hatch. This knowledge drastically changes every situation. Even in a country where the divorce rate hovers around 50 percent, you will have more success with lasting romance if you make a decision to stay together forever than you would if you set out with the intention to "see how it goes." This is especially true if you've already been divorced. You may be tempted to live together before you're legally divorced, but a man who takes marriage seriously won't take *you* seriously until you're legally divorced.

When things were really strained between John and me around the time of our fourth anniversary, I was tempted to walk. But the bond that we shared, forged of faith and conviction, was stronger than that temptation. Instead of leaving, I got busy figuring out what I could do to reclaim the hope and elation we'd felt in the beginning. There were wedding pictures to remind me of my promise and family members and friends to face if I couldn't keep it. Turns out, the power of that sacred vow was great enough to keep me in the marriage.

Thank goodness I found the courage to take the vow in the first place. Otherwise I would have walked away from an absolutely wonderful man.

No matter how long you've been living together or dating, marriage is different—and better.

Instead of playing house, let your urge to live with your man be your motivation to marry him. Having lived with my husband before we were married, I can tell you that marriage is more exciting. I remember feeling unexpectedly giddy and high on our honeymoon in a way that I hadn't experienced on a previous trip we took to Hawaii together. We were both struck with the sense of permanence and depth of the commitment we'd just made. We couldn't stop looking at our new rings and calling each other "my husband" and "my wife." It's a feeling we revisit each year on our anniversary, and on random days when we're reminiscing, or when we're reunited after a few days apart.

The honeymoon euphoria subsided into contentment and satisfaction that sprang from knowing someone loved me enough to say he wanted to be with me forever. This lifted my confidence in a way that just living together never did.

Even sex felt more intimate with the knowledge that we had chosen each other exclusively over all others. Having a lifetime to explore each other's bodies made lovemaking feel luxurious. The best sex comes after you know each other well and trust each other completely. I never experienced that until I married.

For a love that lasts a lifetime, save nothing for the trip back.

# 27

# HONOR YOUR DESIRE TO BE MARRIED, BUT NEVER MAKE ULTIMATUMS

> *Marriage is not a ritual or an end. It is a long, intricate, intimate dance together and nothing matters more than your own sense of balance and your choice of partner.*
>
> —Amy Bloom

*You may be holding up a proposal by sending mixed messages that leave your boyfriend wondering if you'd accept. Examine your subconscious fears to see if you're the one who's stalling.*

*If you're sure you've sent a clear message, and after six months of dating he still hasn't proposed, tell him that while you love him and want to be with him, you're not willing to stay in the relationship if it's not going to lead to wedding bells.*

*This is* not *the same as making an ultimatum such as "Marry me now or I'm leaving you!" An ultimatum is about what he must do, while honoring your desires is about what you must do.*

*A Surrendered Single can't control the outcome of the relationship, so she doesn't try. She hopes for the best but accepts the uncertainty.*

## Send a Consistent Message

If you want a proposal and you've got a longtime lover who's not asking, perhaps *you* are uncertain that he's the one you want "until death do us part." If you've been dating for at least six months, you have all the information you need to make a decision. People tell you who they are immediately, so in just a few months you'll know everything you need to know whether your man is the one for you.

When you're still uncertain that this is *the* right man for you or think you could do better, you unknowingly send him mixed signals. In receiving your signals, your man realizes that if he did propose to you, you might turn him down. So the two of you go along living in relationship limbo, where neither of you truly commits or knows how long it will last. To get out of limbo, find out what you want and send a clear, consistent message.

Ironically, the woman often holds the key to putting the relationship in the next gear. If she wants to get married and sends those signals, she clears the way for her partner to get on his knee and ask for her hand.

# You Hold the Key to the Future of the Relationship

*A journey is like marriage. The certain way to be wrong is to think you control it.*
—John Steinbeck

MaryJane's situation is a good example of how anxieties can sabotage a relationship. Previously divorced with a daughter, she had lived with her boyfriend, Richard, for years. During a workshop she told the group she was frustrated that they weren't married yet, although Richard had proposed years ago. The wedding was always delayed because they didn't have the money to get married in the style that they wanted.

When I suggested that the two of them could run away to elope now and throw a huge party later when they could afford it, MaryJane had a whole new objection. "I'm not sure that I really do want to marry him," she admitted. "I can't believe I'm saying that when all I ever talk about is how I wish we would get married. I thought *he* was the one who was reluctant."

But Richard wasn't reluctant. On further reflection, MaryJane concluded that she did love and want to marry him, but she was afraid that she would get divorced a second time and put her daughter and herself through a trauma. The more she talked about her fears, the more she realized that she was reacting to her past rather than to the loving, committed man in front of her. "I know Richard is a good man and that we could have a wonderful future together," she said.

The other women in the group reflected back to MaryJane her

own confidence that Richard was the right man for her and urged her to find her courage. So with their support, and the knowledge that we were holding her accountable, MaryJane made a decision to face her fears by telling Richard that she wanted to take the next step in their relationship. Instead of worrying about the worst-case scenario, she kept her eye on the ball and summoned the faith to marry a great guy who adored her.

By identifying and addressing her fear in the group, she gave the rest of us the chance to offer perspective. Knowing that we thought her marrying Richard was a good idea helped her move toward the intimacy she yearned for.

Interestingly, when they did get married a few months later, they held a formal ceremony with all their friends in attendance, followed by an elegant dinner—exactly what she had wanted. A friend offered her lovely home for the reception, and another did the catering as a gift. Once she was clear on her intentions, MaryJane found the obstacles that she thought were holding her back not so difficult to overcome.

## Insist on Marriage, but Don't Make a Demand

You can't command anybody to marry you. Even if you could, you'd be cheating yourself out of the thrill of knowing he wants to marry you. You deserve a man who's thinking and acting for himself, a man who decides to marry you because he can't stand the idea of living without you—not because you begged, manipulated, or demanded.

A Surrendered Single doesn't sacrifice her dignity by making such demands of her boyfriend.

On the other hand, you do want to convey to your boyfriend that you would happily agree to marry him if he asked. After all, nobody wants to risk the rejection of being turned down when he proposes. Since you don't want to force his hand by saying, "I would marry you if you asked me," you indicate your willingness through your everyday actions and comments. If he knows that you're happy to see him, think he's smart, find him attractive, and enjoy his touch, then he won't have to wonder how you'll react if he offers you a ring.

Instead of obsessing about whether he's going to marry you, surrender. Focus your energy on yourself and get very clear about what you want and how you feel. If you've been dating for at least three months and things are going well, then it makes sense to tell him that you want to have a husband someday. You don't have to say that you want *him* to be your husband someday, because that would force the issue of whether he feels the same way. Just letting him know that marriage is important to you is enough, because it puts the ball in his court. If he wants to enjoy your company for the rest of his life, he knows he will have to propose.

After you've told him that marriage is in your plans for the future, let it go. You don't have to tell him several times to make sure he gets it. Sometimes just saying something once gives it more weight and significance. It's fine to mention it again if the topic of conversation is "Where do you think you'll be in five years?" But don't go out of your way to make sure he was listening when you told him you want to be a wife.

## Six Months Is Long Enough to Know

*The heart has its reasons which reason knows nothing of.*

—Blaise Pascal

If, at the end of six months, you're no closer to being engaged than you are to being on the moon, then the ball is back in your court. You still can't force or nag him into proposing. However, you can tell him sincerely that while you love him and want to be with him, you need to be married. If that doesn't fit for him, tell him that you need to move on. Then it's up to him to decide if he will let you go or become the man who agrees to love, honor, and protect you.

If he says he's not ready to get married, you can either give up on ever having a wedding or else leave him and make room in your life for a man who would be thrilled to say "I do."

When you stay with a man who doesn't want to marry you, you're cheating yourself out of being pursued and cherished the way you deserve to be. The low-level agony and anxiety you will feel from knowing that you aren't getting what you want may seem less painful than the dramatic sting of a breakup, but over time the effect is no less torturous.

You might be tempted to wait longer, thinking he needs more time. It may not sound like much time, but six months of dating is long enough to know whether or not you want to commit to someone for life. That doesn't mean he has to be willing to elope with you that instant, only that he is willing to make plans to marry in the future. That future may be at the end of medical school or after his daughter leaves for college next year. The time frame isn't all that important, as long as there *is* a time frame.

Sometimes a man will tell you shortly after you start dating that he doesn't believe in marriage or doesn't plan to marry ever. Naturally, you might be inclined to take his word for it. However, men are a bit peculiar this way, because they sometimes say things like that and then completely change their minds once they fall in love. Lots of men are not commitment oriented until they meet the woman they can't live without.

So how can you tell before six months if a man will eventually commit to you? Unfortunately, you can't. It takes that long to build the kind of bond that will make a man want to keep you in his life permanently. More important, you need that long to decide whether you're with a man that *you* could be happy with for many years to come.

## Take Care of Yourself and the Ring May Follow

> *You don't marry someone you can live with—you marry the person who you cannot live without.*
>
> —Anonymous

Telling a man you must move on when a proposal is lacking is not manipulating him into marriage; it's good self-care. The former is a veiled threat, while the latter is about saying what fits for you. Saying "I respect that your needs are different from mine, and I have to take care of myself by moving on," is focused on changing the only thing you can—yourself. Saying "If you don't marry me,

I'm going to leave!" is focused on what he must do and is an attempt to control. That is no way to start a life together.

Sometimes the realization that he's about to lose you for good will make a man reconsider his commitment to permanent bachelorhood and prompt him to propose, as in Georgia's case.

Georgia's boyfriend, Nathan, not only bought her a ring, he married her—but on an island in Tahiti, in a marriage that is not recognized in the United States. They had planned to make it legal upon returning from their honeymoon. Instead, Nathan's business partner pressured him to put it off until their startup company was more established. The couple was already living together when Georgia tried pleading, begging, demanding, insisting, and threatening Nathan to go through with a second, legal wedding. He resisted her efforts mightily. The sore subject put such a strain on their relationship that it threatened to destroy it. Then Georgia took a new tack.

"I understand that your business is very important to you, and I respect that," she told him firmly without crying. "I also know that to be happy, I need to get married. I need that commitment. I love you and I want to be your wife, but if it's not the right thing for you, I can accept that—and move on."

When Nathan didn't say anything immediately, Georgia's heart leapt into her throat. A few minutes later, he turned to her and said, "Things are going so well for us lately. I don't want to lose you, so we've got to take care of this problem. We'll be married by March."

Georgia had been willing to do just what she said, even though she would have been heartbroken to lose Nathan. There was no empty threat or anger in her words. She stayed focused on herself and her own limits, which is just the opposite of an ultimatum that demands that *he* do something—or else. Had she said, "Either we get married or else I'm leaving you," his response would likely have been very different. Anger, not affection, is the natural response to a controlling ultimatum. As it was, she told Nathan just the facts—

that she loved him and respected herself too much to stay in a situation that didn't meet her deepest needs.

Although Georgia made herself very vulnerable in this situation, she was also showing tremendous dignity. What she did was incredibly strong, and that wasn't lost on Nathan. Who wouldn't be attracted to someone with so much self-respect?

Monica and Pete kept separate apartments even though they had been dating for over a year. At that point, Monica realized that while she hoped he would propose soon, he was making no signs of it. Although she was deeply in love with him, she decided that if he was not the marrying type, she would be better off leaving him and finding someone she could marry. She prepared to tell him what she needed and steeled herself against the possibility of having to end the relationship.

On the way home from an enjoyable evening together, she said, "Peter, I love you so much, but I don't want to just keep dating forever. I'd like to be able to take our relationship to the next level. If you're not ready to do that, or that's not where you're headed, I understand, but I know that's what I want and need to be happy."

Peter, who hadn't been contemplating marriage at all, was surprised. He pulled over to the side of the road to think for a moment. Then he said, "I want to get married." He paused again. "I want to get married to you." Finally, as he realized it for the first time, he said, "I want to marry you now!" He proposed to her on the spot.

These stories—and many others I know—had happy endings, largely because of the way these wise women delivered their messages. No one can guarantee that your boyfriend will respond the same way, but there is plenty you can do to improve your odds.

## Honoring Your Desires Is Not the Same as Making an Ultimatum

So what is the difference between what Georgia and Monica said and giving a man an ultimatum? There are five elements to effectively communicating and honoring your desires in the area of marriage:

- **Make no demands.** Georgia and Monica said what was true for them, but did *not* insist that their men take a specific action or else suffer threatened consequences.
- **Be calm.** Both conversations were serious, but neither woman delivered her message in anger, frustration, or tears.
- **Admit you love him.** This may be difficult because it feels so vulnerable, but it's important to tell him that you think he's the one for you. It's possible that he has been holding back because he is afraid that you will reject his proposal. If he has not yet professed that he loves you when you're ready to have this conversation, then simply substitute "I want to be with you," so you don't risk any more than necessary.
- **Wait for a good time.** Both of the aforementioned relationships were going well when the topic was brought up. It wasn't right after a fight or amid weeks of bickering.
- **Be willing to follow through.** Georgia and Monica were prepared to give up relationships they treasured in order to give themselves the chance to have what they deeply desired. Without that piece, their words would have been a manipulation, rather than a statement of truth.

Before you deliver a similar message to your boyfriend, you too will want to wait for the right moment, consider your phrasing carefully, and stay calm.

Most important though, you will have to muster the conviction to leave the relationship if he is unwilling to make a commitment. If you aren't ready to follow through on your announcement, your boyfriend will sense it on some level. He may dismiss what you're saying as not that important, since it lacks real consequences for him.

You may need some time to prepare yourself mentally before you talk to your boyfriend. However, you would betray yourself by going month after month without bringing up the important topic of what you need to be happy. You might be having a great time with your boyfriend, but if he can't meet your future needs, those good times will soon deteriorate into tension and bickering. Find the courage to address the situation with dignity, and you will have a better chance of getting everything you want.

If you express your need to be married and your willingness to move on if necessary and he still doesn't ask you to be his wife, you would be betraying yourself to stay in that relationship. Your respect for yourself and his regard for you will drop proportionally. By all means, enter the conversation hoping for the best, but be prepared for the worst.

## Surrender for a Month Before Bringing Up a Sore Subject

If the issue of marriage has come up in your relationship before and is a source of contention, you may be wondering how you're ever going to find a good time to bring this up again. Sometimes this point alone is enough to cause a relationship to deteriorate, which further reinforces everyone's fears that maybe this isn't a match made in heaven. If you've been haranguing your boyfriend, making sarcastic comments, or criticizing him for his lack of commitment and the tension is thick, then you'll need to change your behavior for one month before you bring this subject up again.

For thirty days, be as loving and as surrendered as you can. Even if you are resentful, angry, and scared that he'll never marry you, you will need to act in faith that everything's going to turn out fine. Do this to give the relationship a fair chance and to remind you both why you wanted to be together in the first place.

During that month, make it a priority to respect him and apologize when you haven't been so respectful. Avoid nagging, criticizing, or trying to control him. I'm not suggesting that you would make his favorite dinner every night or buy him presents. That's not sustainable behavior and could cause you to be resentful. Rather, just concentrate on doing your part to make the union a harmonious one. That way, when you tell him what it is you truly need, marriage will be in the realm of possibility.

I know a month doesn't seem like very long, but it is plenty long enough for him to see a glimpse of his future with you. It's long enough to forget that a month ago you were fighting constantly. It's long enough to lay the foundation for a happy ending to the conversation.

## Making a Monkey of Yourself by Hanging On

We've all heard stories about some woman who dated or lived with a guy for nine years who just wouldn't marry her. Assuming she really was willing to commit to him, it's tempting to blame it all on the jerk she was with. In reality, the woman herself betrayed her own desires by staying when her needs were not being met. Six months into that relationship, she had all the information she needed to decide if she wanted to marry him. So if a couple goes for nine years without any progress toward that end, then the woman was doing what I've done many times in my life: holding on to something that wasn't right for me because I thought it was better than nothing.

This reminds me of a method of catching monkeys in the wild, which I understand is very easy to do with a box and a grapefruit. The monkey sees the box with the grapefruit in it and reaches his hand through a small hole to grab it. Then he is unable to pull his hand and the grapefruit out of the box because the hole is too small. Still, once he has the grapefruit, the monkey won't let go, and his captors can easily scoop him up.

Holding on to the wrong man because you think he's better than nothing is just like the monkey clutching the grapefruit. It's a trap. We can imagine how sweet it will be to have the marriage we're dreaming of, but we can't actually enjoy it, which is maddening. Walking away hurts like hell, but only temporarily. It also frees you up to spend your energy on self-care and attracting a man who knows he wants you as his wife.

You may worry that it will take forever to attract the right man, since it took so long to meet the one you have now. But if you apply what you've learned from this book, it won't take long to meet the man who's right for you. There are plenty of single men out there, and you can go out with them and enjoy those possibilities as soon as you get out of the dead-end relationship you're in.

You might feel more comfortable staying in a predictable but unsatisfying relationship than risking the uncertainty of dating new men. But the price of staying with a man who won't make you his wife is too high. A Surrendered Single finds the courage to leave a man who can never make her happy in favor of the unknown. That is the one thing she can change about her situation.

## Angling for a Proposal Will Slow Down the Process

Patty had been dating Matt for nearly five years and was frustrated that he hadn't proposed. "I tell him all the time that he better get me a ring," she said. Naturally, Matt was making no moves toward getting a ring, because he didn't want to be controlled into getting one.

He *did* want to make long-term plans with her—including making a will so that she would be protected if anything happened to him and adopting her daughter—but because of Patty's constant nagging, Matt would not discuss marriage. Perhaps he wanted to, but in his own time and in his own way. Patty gave him no chance to do this.

As soon as she realized that she had made it virtually impossible for him to propose without feeling completely emasculated, she made a conscious decision to back off. To compensate for her controlling comments in the past, she focused on her boyfriend's good qualities and avoided marriage, proposals, rings, or anything related. She realized that her years of constant nagging and bickering about this sore subject had worked against her and wisely reasoned that doing the opposite might help. Patty decided to wait this one out for several months to see what happened. Within a month, Matt brought up the topic of matrimony at the breakfast table in a very positive way. "I don't think we need a long engagement, do you?" he asked. Patty simply smiled at him, amazed. This reaction from Matt was so encouraging, she was able to keep her promise to herself to refrain from making any marriage-related comments for another two months.

By then he was on one knee, asking her to marry him.

If you have a sense that your boyfriend *does* want to marry you and you have nagged, cajoled, and cried about getting married, do your best to let go of the whole topic for at least three months. As with all surrendering, you can't control the outcome. However, your chance of getting what you want increases dramatically when you stop trying to force his hand and let him make up his own mind.

## Sometimes It's Okay to Wait

Maggie was feeling some desperation about her future with Daniel. She knew from previous conversations that while he was completely devoted to her, he was also focused on finishing his law degree before he got engaged. On a hunch, Maggie made a conscious decision to wait for him for the next two years, deciding that this was a worthwhile gamble for her. Sure enough, when graduation was over, he not only proposed to her, he thanked her for being willing to wait for him.

Maggie's decision had been a gift to both of them. Not only was Daniel able to focus on school without worrying that he would lose Maggie, she was able to relax and enjoy her boyfriend for the two years instead of bickering about when they would get engaged. At the end of the two years, he was more in love with her than ever.

You may be wondering if your situation, like Maggie's, warrants waiting. Before you decide, first check with your intuition to see if you feel that this relationship has a wonderful, wedded future. If you feel that it does, ask yourself how long you need to wait for him. Think about whether you can actually wait that long and *not* feel resentful if the relationship never advances. Finally, be sure you take care of yourself while you're waiting. (Maggie did not pay for his tuition or live with him during the two years.)

Anyone who waits for a man who never marries her would be

disappointed, but if you suspect you would also feel resentment, then you can't afford to take the wager. Only you know for sure what's right for your situation.

Sometimes the prospect of becoming a husband will incite a man to make changes in his work. If your beloved wants to finish his education or land a new job before he gets married, it may be that he is preparing himself to be a groom. Ken's story illustrates this point. Gabriella, his bride-to-be, was stunned when he left his job the day before the wedding. Ken seemed confident and resolute when he explained that his employers were taking advantage of him and that the lack of challenge and room for growth left him feeling emasculated. "I couldn't be the kind of man you deserve while I was working there," he told her. "I want to be stronger and more ambitious than that so I can be a better husband."

If your boyfriend wants to advance his career or education before he commits, it could be that he's preparing for marriage, not running from it. The only way to tell is to listen to him carefully and see what he reveals.

A Surrendered Single knows she can't control the timing of a proposal, so she doesn't try. She sets limits that she can accept while maintaining good self-care. She finds the courage to act on her conviction, because she knows that it will lead her to the relationship she's always wanted.

disappointment, but if you suspect you would also feel resentment, then you can't afford to take the wager. Only you know for sure what's right for your situation.

Sometimes the prospect of becoming a husband will incite a man to make changes in his work. If your beloved wants to finish his education or land a new job before he gets married, it may be that he is preparing himself to be a groom. Ken's story illustrates this point. Gabriella, his bride-to-be, was stunned when he left his job the day before the wedding. Ken seemed confident and resolute when he explained that his employers were taking advantage of him and that the lack of challenge and room for growth left him feeling unsatisfied. "I couldn't be the kind of man you deserve while I was working there," he told her. "I want to be stronger and more ambitious than that so I can be a better husband."

If your boyfriend wants to advance his career or education before he commits, it could be that he's preparing for marriage, not running from it. The only way to tell is to listen to him carefully and see what he reveals.

A Surrendered Single knows she can't control the timing of a proposal, so she doesn't try. She sets limits that she can accept while maintaining good self-care. She finds the courage to act on her conviction, because she knows that it will lead her to the relationship she's always wanted.

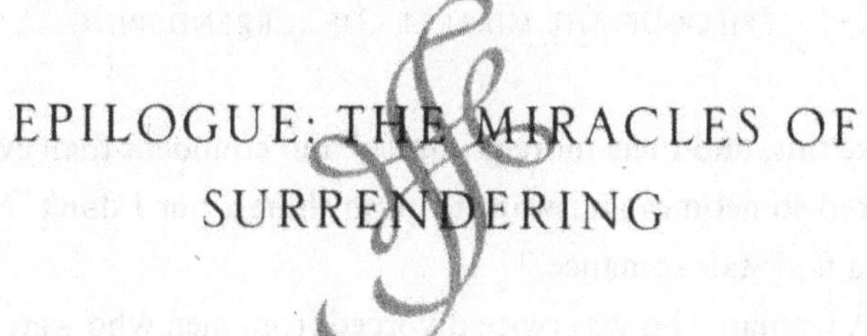

# EPILOGUE: THE MIRACLES OF SURRENDERING

> *Love cures people, both the ones who give it and the ones who receive it.*
>
> —Dr. Karl A. Menninger

I've been privileged to watch some wonderful romances blossom for formerly cynical, hopeless women who had enough faith to apply the principles of the Surrendered Single. Here are some of the things I witnessed:

- A woman who hadn't dated in ages and felt desperate and hopeless reluctantly joined an online dating service. Soon she had lots of dating offers, and she accepted several of them. Now she was dating again, but everything was different because she was dating the surrendered way. She felt more confident and beautiful. Suddenly, men around her—not just the ones from the dating service—were pursuing her, too. For the first time in years, she was part of the dating scene, and she was enjoying it.
- A woman told our singles group that she had ruled out dating a friend of a friend because he wasn't as tall as she would have liked. When we encouraged her to stay open to the possibilities, she found that she delighted in his company. They began dating steadily. She had wanted to call him to get reassurance and to find out when she would see him again, but she thought better of it and didn't. "This is so different for me," she reported. "I've never let a relationship unfold natu-

rally like this, and I feel more grounded and confident than ever. I still get scared sometimes and want to push things, but I don't. Now I'm having a fairy-tale romance."

- A woman who was twice divorced from men who weren't good guys couldn't imagine ever trusting a man enough to fall in love again. Still, she was willing to make herself available in the hopes that she could. Nine weeks after she started dating surrendered-style, a blind date turned into a wonderful love affair. She was tempted to talk a lot on the first date, but she didn't. "This is the most comforting feeling I have had with a man in a long time," she told me. "You only have to be in the room with a good guy for five minutes to know that you didn't have a good guy before." Her boyfriend complimented her by saying, "You've shown me that women can communicate and not manipulate."
- A woman in our group met her beau when she started smiling at everyone she saw. "Even though I'm fifty-five and have been married more than once, I feel like I've never had a real relationship before," she reported. "I'm learning to be playful and laugh, not to manipulate things. It feels wonderful!"
- A woman who started surrendering long after she met and became engaged to her boyfriend told me how wonderful her eight-month-old marriage is. "Remember just last year you weren't sure if he was the right man for you?" I teased her. She looked surprised. "I said that?" she asked. "I can't believe it. I never think that now. He's definitely the perfect man for me."

Many women commented that when they surrendered, the relationships seemed to develop more slowly than what they were used to. This was probably because they weren't racing to get to the next milestone to ease fears.

Although I wasn't surprised, it was magical to see that when women in the group surrendered, they not only attracted wonderful men, but they also developed relationships that helped them heal wounds they didn't even know they had. It was as though the right man for each came equipped with the very quality that she most needed in her life.

For example, one woman's past disappointments had led her to believe—perhaps only subconsciously—that she could be lovable only if she was sexual. She had always used sex to connect with men right away. So when her boyfriend purposely resisted sexual contact between them for months because he was really serious about her and wanted to get to know her, she wondered. Was he gay or uninterested? No. He was clearly attracted to her and courted her like crazy, but he had decided to take things slowly.

"On the one hand, I'm dying to have sex with him!" she told me. "On the other hand, I know I'm not ready.

"Getting to know him first without being sexual is scary. I guess I never believed before that a man would hang around with me if I wasn't giving him sex. He is showing me that I am lovable for who I am without that," she marveled. "I never dreamed this would happen, but I know it's just what I needed. I'm learning that I'm just an old-fashioned girl, but I never knew it before."

Another woman was anxious about letting her boyfriend pay for everything on a date, because she knew he didn't have a lot of money. "I feel so anxious when he takes out his credit card to pay for dinner, because I know he's going into debt. So finally I offered to pay for something, and he just smiled and said, 'I've got it. Don't worry—you're worth it.' I started crying, because I was raised believing that I needed to take care of myself at all times, and it turns out I don't have to. I'm forty-one and I've never felt that I was worth someone taking care of me like that—until now."

Another woman who was also used to fending for herself joked with her new boyfriend about how much time they were spending together when she said, "Why don't we just move in?"

"I'd love to," he replied. "But I don't think you'd be comfortable doing that, and I want you to be comfortable."

She was speechless. It was more considerate than anything she'd experienced before from a man. True, she had already told him that she wouldn't be comfortable living together without a sacred commitment, but she was surprised that he remembered and would uphold it on her behalf. "Instead of trying to get what he wants, he's all about making sure I'm happy. It was so disarming. I always think I have to protect myself at all times, and here he is protecting me like I'm the most precious thing."

Where these women thought their worth was based on sex or self-sufficiency, or that they had to be vigilant in protecting their interests, they were blessed with men who showed them just the opposite was true. In each case, we were amazed that the woman got *exactly* the kind of treatment she needed to move past her own injury. It was magical.

For some women, surrendering meant the end of the relationship they were already in. For instance, one woman was feeling taken advantage of and decided to start practicing self-care, expressing her desires, and receiving more from her boyfriend of five months. Only two weeks later, he told her he didn't love her anymore. Reflecting on the relationship, she realized that she had arranged her life around him—even initiated the first date—while he had made playing soccer his priority. "I think I was convenient for him until I started having wants, and then he thought I was too much trouble. That's not what I want in a man," she admitted. Although the breakup was disappointing, she realized that surrendering had helped her eliminate a man who hadn't been treating her well.

Fortunately, using surrendering techniques from day one increases the chances that you'll attract the kind of man you want, rather than one that you'll have to break up with later. You don't have to apply them perfectly to enjoy the benefits, either. A friend of mine discovered this when she met a man who broke through her defenses. "I tried to make myself available, but I wasn't perfect at it.

It didn't matter, because he was determined to win me over, which felt great. I loved hearing from him that he'd waited for me all his life, how much he adored me, and how beautiful I was. I did my best to receive his compliments graciously, even though they made me squirm at times," she admitted. She received and accepted the biggest compliment of all when he asked her to marry him.

Perhaps the best thing about surrendered dating is that it establishes habits early on that will contribute to a long and happy marriage. I know of no better way to not only divorce-proof your marriage, but to keep it full of passion and intimacy. And the only way to do that is to relinquish control of that which you cannot control; in other words to control only yourself.

I know this sounds like a pie-in-the-sky promise. But in my work with thousands of wives, I've found that ordinary couples can overcome every kind of conflict to stay married and find happiness as long as the husband is a good guy and the wife doesn't try to control him. I've seen couples overcome minor annoyances, such as temporary unemployment, living in cramped quarters, or dealing with hectic work schedules, as well as conflicts that seemed insurmountable—severe financial hardship, sickness, or the loss of a child. In every case, the couples were able to find companionship, stability, tenderness, and intimacy.

You will also find these things with a man who's right for you—as soon as you begin surrendering.

# ABOUT THE AUTHOR

Laura Doyle is the author of the *New York Times* bestseller *The Surrendered Wife: A Practical Guide to Finding Intimacy, Passion, and Peace with a Man* (Fireside, 2001). Doyle leads Surrendered workshops for singles and wives and speaks to women about how to find and keep intimate, passionate relationships.

Once a copywriter for a marketing firm, Doyle earned her journalism degree from San Jose State University. She lives in Costa Mesa, California, with John Doyle, her husband of twelve years.

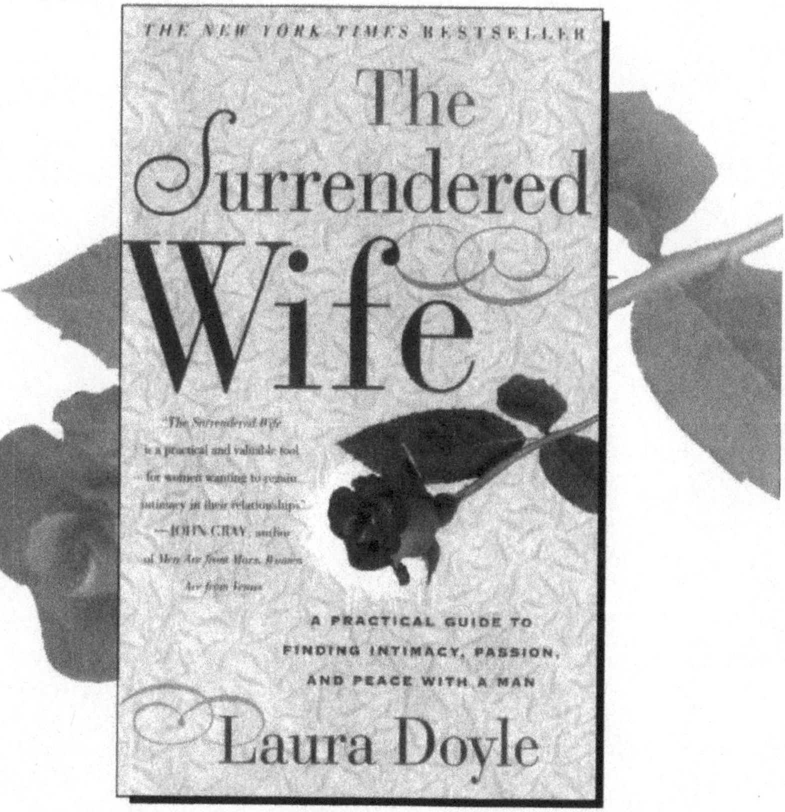